MW00414319

THE
FORGOTTEN
CHOICE

Also by Brenda Bence

Leading YOU™

Would YOU Want to Work for YOU™?

Master the Brand Called YOU™

Brand Yourself a Leader

Branding Matters

Smarter Branding Without Breaking the Bank

How YOU™ *Are Like Shampoo for Job Seekers*

How YOU™ *Are Like Shampoo for College Graduates*

How YOU™ *Are Like Shampoo*

The Power of the Platform (Contributing Author)

Praise from around the world for *The Forgotten Choice*

"*The Forgotten Choice* is a powerful guide to how you can create real, lasting behavioral change—beginning with your mindset and ending in life-long habits. With excellent writing and engaging storytelling, Bence makes you reflect on the way you perceive your life and how you can use the tools you already have to change the things that hold you back from success. A must read!"

> — Marshall Goldsmith, Thinkers 50 #1 Executive Coach and only two-time #1 Leadership Thinker in the world

"*The Forgotten Choice* is one of the best guides around for redirecting your perspective on life, creating what you want, and being happy with what you have. Author Brenda Bence's warm, comforting writing style is crisp, trustworthy and spot-on, resulting in a rapid, easy read."

> — Starred Review, *BlueInk Reviews*

"*The Forgotten Choice* is one of those rare books that, with a new way of seeing what we do every day, can change the course of one's life. If you feel powerless to change anything that is not quite right in your life, let *The Forgotten Choice* give you back the power."

> — Marianna Pascal, Top 100 TEDx Speaker Worldwide

"Enlightening, inspirational, and self-empowering advice … riveting …"

> — "Get it!" Review, *Kirkus Reviews*

'*The Forgotten Choice* is more than a self-help book. It is a book that will ιelp the reader to live life on their terms, craft their present and future, nd make sure their life is what they want it to be."

> — 5-Star Rating, *Readers' Favorite Reviews*

love this original and inspiring book. It challenges you to think about urself and motivates you to transform your perception and see the ›rld full of opportunities. Absolutely wonderful and a must read!"

> — Krista Baetens, Executive Asia, Corporate & Institutional Banking, NAB

"I began reading Brenda Bence's book, *The Forgotten Choice*, in the afternoon and didn't stop until I had read it from cover to cover! The many real-life examples Brenda shared demonstrate her principles and processes in practice and make them so applicable. What a wonderful book!"

— Mike Maloney, Author of *Choosing to be Gay*

"This book was empowering and engaging. I will be recommending it to everyone!"

— Julie Schmidt, Vice President of Finance and Administration and Treasurer, Doane University

"*The Forgotten Choice* is more than just a useful reminder. It's an encouraging guide to thoughtful action—and to action in your thoughts. Brilliant!"

— Ron Kaufman, *New York Times* bestselling author of *Uplifting Service*

"The beauty of *The Forgotten Choice* is its simplicity. The examples are engaging, and the techniques are practical and easily applied in both personal and professional settings. I will be sure to recommend *The Forgotten Choice*."

— Gordon Cameron, Head of Ex US Divestitures, Takeda

"Rooted in theory, yet steeped in practical examples and straightforward approaches, readers of *The Forgotten Choice* will learn how to reclaim their infinite potential on the way to creating their preferred futures. A must read for those who want to regain purpose and control of their lives."

— Dr. Susan Fritz, University of Nebraska Executive Vice President and Provost

"The concept in *The Forgotten Choice* is game changing. It's so simple to understand, but precisely because it is so simple, it is immediately applicable. What a good book!"

— Chin Yoke Yew, Lead Consultant, Paradigm Auditing and Consulting

"Lessons from *The Forgotten Choice* helped me to reframe my mindset pyramid and my approach to creating the future. This is a book I will keep tucked in my digital pocket as a reminder to never forget this choice."

— Toni M. Ganzel, MD, MBA, Vice President of Academic Medical Affairs, Dean of the School of Medicine, Professor of Otolaryngology-Head and Neck Surgery, University of Louisville

THE
FORGOTTEN
CHOICE

SHIFT YOUR INNER MINDSET, SHAPE YOUR OUTER WORLD

BRENDA BENCE

Global
Insight

Published by Global Insight Communications LLC, Las Vegas, Nevada, U.S.A.
ISBN: 978-1-942718-07-9
Library of Congress Control Number: 2020902500

Editor and contributor: Sherri Rothenberger
Editors: Melanie Votaw, Jessi Rita Hoffman
Interior design and typesetting by Eric Myhr
Graphics by Swas "Kwan" Siripong
Photos by Bergen Johnston and Danielle Johnston

Unless otherwise noted, the stories in this book are based on real events and real people. To protect the privacy of individuals and companies, names and identifying details have been changed.

Unless otherwise noted, all footnoted webpage references were last accessed in September 2020.

Publisher's Cataloging-in-Publication Data:

Names: Bence, Brenda S., author.
Title: The forgotten choice : shift your inner mindset, shape your outer world Brenda Bence.
Description: Las Vegas, NV: Global Insight Communications, LLC, 2021.
Identifiers: LCCN: 2020902500 | ISBN: 978-1-942718-07-9
Subjects: LCSH Success. | Success--Psychological aspects. | Belief and doubt Self-actualization (Psychology) | Change (Psychology) | Behavior modificatic | Performance--Psychological aspects. | BISAC SELF-HELP / Personal Grow / Success
Classification: LCC BF773 .B46 F67 2021 | DDC 153.8--dc23

Dedicated to
the Joy of Possibility

Contents

Introduction:
The Forgotten Choice

Picture a pack of runners preparing for a cross-country race, and split them into two groups. The night before the race, you give one group of runners a map of the trail, showing them where they will run and what to expect. You tell the second group to show up on the morning of the race and figure out where to go by following the signs along the trail. Which group will end up with faster race times? The group that had the map beforehand. Why?

We're hard-wired for certainty. We like predictability, so when we know what to expect, we feel safe, we're more confident, and we get better results.

In life, there are moments when we *do* feel confident, safe and secure, on a "high." But then, something unexpected appears out of nowhere—an important relationship ends abruptly, your boss tells you your job is on the line, a competitor dramatically drops their price, or a previously unknown virus spreads through the world threatening lives. The result? Uncertainty rears its ugly head again, leaving us feeling powerless, weak, and tired.

As if on a rollercoaster, this pattern of ups and downs repeats itself, day after day, month after month. While most of us love the fast drops of a rollercoaster at an amusement park, it's the last thing we want in our everyday lives.

During times of uncertainty, it's key to focus on what's permanent, reliable, and unchanging—the constants in life. This book will reveal one of the most important constants that is available to you at any moment: the forgotten choice.

Once you remember it, this choice will allow you to permanently get off of the daily rollercoaster. And it will help you not just in times of uncertainty, but when faced with frustration, irritation, disgust, anger, grief, or any general sense of unease. Whatever challenges you face, the forgotten choice can help you get back to a place of feeling good again, of taking charge of your future.

The forgotten choice is 100% reliable—a choice we've always had available to us, but one that most of us don't remember. The problem is that we've been looking for solutions in the wrong place. Because what will truly improve our lives isn't *outside* of us. It isn't *doing* that creates change. No, the answer lies in *being*—in shifting our *inner mindset*—and that's what actually shapes our outer world.

Unfortunately, we aren't taught the fundamental truth that it is our mindset, consisting of our thoughts and beliefs, that drives what happens to us every day. Shaping a better life on the outside starts with how we think on the inside, and yet we woefully—and consistently—underestimate the power of our thoughts.

As a result, we play small, failing to recognize that we can control more of what happens in our daily lives than we realize. But in order to take that control, we have to shift the way we think and challenge the long-held beliefs that have stood in our way. One of the greatest management minds of all time, Peter Drucker, said, "The best way to predict the future is to create it." And that's exactly what this book will show you how to do.

This foundational choice isn't just about "positive versus negative thinking." As you'll learn, it's something much more powerful and fundamental than that. And if this sounds mystical or like some sort of "magical thinking," I assure you it's not. As you'll discover on the pages that follow, this concept is absolutely consistent with recent discoveries of modern science.

The Evolution of *The Forgotten Choice*

As the owner of a successful, global leadership coaching practice and international keynote speaking business, I coach people every week who are senior-level leaders working for large, multinational corporations. These individuals are all smart, driven, and extremely successful. Yet, despite their tremendous achievements, it's not unusual for them to tell me they feel limited—that they are not living up to their full potential and are not as satisfied or happy as they would like to be.

For years, in the pursuit of my own personal growth, I studied the power of thoughts and beliefs and the impact they have on the outcomes of our lives. I put this learning into practice, and as I'll share in this book, the results I experienced were nothing short of miraculous.

So I began to wonder: could the techniques I'd developed for myself help my executive coaching clients, too?

I started sharing a concept or two with clients, and one by one, they also began to experience amazing outcomes.

That success prompted me to broaden my sharing with staff members, family, and eventually with audiences, too, both large and small—people from all walks of life and from all around the globe. Everywhere I taught these concepts, the results were transformational.

As of today, I've had the joy of sharing what you'll read in this book with audiences and clients from more than one hundred countries, demonstrating that these concepts are absolutely universal and bring equally outstanding results for all. Given the incredible outcomes that I and others were seeing and experiencing from regularly remembering the forgotten choice, I was inspired to broaden its reach even further. That's how this book came to be.

Here's the Plan

We'll begin by looking at the big picture of where we are now, how we all got here, and how the hidden influences of history caused us to forget this oh-so-critical choice which impacts us every single day.

Then, you'll learn how to use an eye-opening process that will turn your current understanding of cause and effect on its head. You'll realize that you are more in charge of the events of your life than you may have ever believed.

You'll get clear on how to consistently choose between two intangible yet opposite thought-systems that form the forgotten choice, and you'll learn how regularly embracing one of these will get you the outcomes you desire.

Lastly, you'll get crystal clear on the life you really *do* want and learn how to take daily steps toward turning that desire into reality.

Once you begin to master the forgotten choice, life becomes an outright adventure, filled with a sense of curiosity and freedom. Throughout this book, I will guide you step-by-step to a clear understanding of the forgotten choice and how to leverage it to make powerful, positive changes in your life and work.

If you're ready for this kind of change, turn the page, and let's get started.

— 1 —

The Choice You Make
Every Moment

Every day, from the minute we wake up until the time we go to bed, we are called on to make decisions—hundreds, if not thousands of little and not-so-little choices confront us daily. Many of our decisions can feel trivial, seeming to have little serious impact on our quality of life. Others, involving career, relationships, parenting, or health, seem to carry much more importance.

Even though the incredibly tough decisions don't present themselves every day—such as whether to end a relationship, start your own business, or buy or sell a house—none of us are immune from having to make big decisions.

Every time we make a choice—large or small—we are unknowingly aligning with one of two separate and distinct thought-systems: one which is founded in fear, and the other which is founded in what I call the "Joy of Possibility."

This book will help you recognize the impact these two thought-systems have on every aspect of your daily life. It will bring to your awareness the tremendous ability you have to consciously choose the Joy of Possibility over fear, in order to create the life you want. **This is the forgotten choice.**

We all love choice and even feel empowered by it. **Yet, every minute of every day, we overlook this most important choice.**

Even though this choice is the single-most powerful decision we can make, we haven't been taught how to use it. We subconsciously reject it in favor of old, historic, programmed beliefs that don't serve us anymore.

This book will not only help you understand the forgotten choice but, more importantly, it will show you how to remember it regularly and use it to make positive, long-term changes. When we do this consciously and consistently, we begin to experience a higher level of satisfaction in all areas of our lives, including relationships, work, finances, and family life, just to name a few.

But in order for that to happen, let's step back for a bit, and look at where we've been and where we are as a human race. That will put this all-important choice into context.

— 2 —

Why We're Not All
Dancing in the Streets

The lives we lead today were nothing but daydreams for our not-so-distant ancestors. Pause and reflect on what someone from just a few generations back would think if they were a fly on the wall, observing how we live. The idea of a daily, hot shower in a modern bathroom, sitting on a comfortable couch watching a television, or picking up a cell phone and calling anyone anywhere in the world would have been unheard of. Accustomed to cooking over open fires or coal stoves, our ancestors would marvel at even the most modest kitchens today, not to mention a refrigerator linked to your smartphone that can complete your grocery list. Most of our everyday problems are easily solved by a Google search or a quick chat with Siri. The revolution that technology has brought us in the twenty-first century is nothing short of astounding.

And it isn't just technology. We've evolved culturally and socially, too, and have experienced astonishing breakthroughs in health and medicine that we often take for granted. Our existence is so radically different from our ancestors' that our life expectancy has now more than doubled, from an estimated 40 years of age back in 1918 to 100+ years in many countries.[1] Compared to our ancestors, children born today are actually getting *more than two lifetimes in one.*

So, we are living longer, better-quality lives than ever in the history of humankind. We are evolving at a remarkably rapid pace. We have a long list of amazing technological advances that make our daily lives so much easier. And we have a longer time to enjoy all of this while we are here.

Then why are we not all dancing in the streets with joy?

I wanted to find out just how we view this miraculous world we live in and how we would describe our existence today. I set up an online survey and made a request, followed by one simple question: "Pause and reflect on the state of the world today from a political, economic, social, and emotional standpoint. Now consider this: if the world were a person, what five descriptive words/adjectives would you use to describe that person right now? Fill in the blanks: 'I would describe that person as _____ , _____ , _____ , _____ , and _____ .'"

Thousands of comments were sent in from thirty-four countries across six continents. The results? Almost 70% of the words were negative. The most frequent entries were some form of "confused, conflicted, angry, selfish, unpredictable, sad, uncertain, and fearful." In summary, we live this amazing, never-experienced-

---

1.   Elizabeth Arias, Ph.D. and Jiaguan Yu, M.D., "United States Life Tables, 2017," National Vital Statistics Reports 68, no. 7, June 24, 2019, accessed September 16, 2020, https://www.cdc.gov/nchs/data/nvsr/nvsr68/nvsr68_07-508.pdf, 46, 48.

before existence, and yet most of us perceive the world as a negative place. Why?

I believe it's because we tend to look outside of ourselves for how to make our lives better. We look to the tangible to solve our problems and bring us happiness. We look to the things we buy, to spouses or significant others, to money, to politicians, to new laws, to the latest new gadget. We say, "If only I had more money, if I could afford a nicer home, if I were in better physical shape. If I could just find more capable employees, if my spouse would just be more thoughtful, if our kids would just behave, if we weren't spending sleepless nights worrying about our aging parents, if I could just get that promotion, if… [fill in the blank with your own answer here], *then,* I would have a truly great, stress-free life." The problem, it seems, is that for us to have the lives of our dreams, everyone and everything outside of us has to change.

Since we believe our problems are coming from outside us, we also look outside of ourselves for solutions. We look to others for validation, acceptance, and appreciation. We look to our diplomas, careers, finances, homes, cars, and clothes to give us a sense of status and worth. Perhaps we adopt the latest nutrition fad or fitness craze, or we follow a guru. We've become so focused externally that we gauge our success based on how many "likes" or "retweets" we just received. Is it any wonder we live in a world where we see the glass as half empty?

Whenever we believe that responsibility for our lives rests outside of ourselves, we place control in someone else's hands. Then, when we don't get the outcomes we desire, we end up playing the blame game. We point to other people or things as the source of our misery—to governments, corporate greed, entitlement programs, the rich, the poor, or to people with different political or religious beliefs. This way of thinking leads us to see ourselves as victims.

Clearly, based on the survey results, this external focus is not working. Deep inside, we know we're looking in the wrong place, but we keep focusing externally anyway, in hopes that it will eventually change our lives for the better. What's driving that?

I think the answer lies in one of the single-most important events that has happened in recorded history. Occurring about 100 years ago, this incident had the potential to completely alter how we look at life. But within a relatively short period, it was glossed over and shelved, shuffled quietly onto the back burner of history.

The lead-up to that event and the reason why it's been glossed over make up one of the most fascinating chapters of our human history.

— 3 —

How Intangibles Became Taboo

I t all began with a famous apple incident—but not the Steve Jobs kind nor the Garden of Eden variety. The apple I'm referring to is the one that fell out of a tree some 300 years ago and landed on the head of an English mathematician and physicist, Isaac Newton. Considered one of the greatest scientists of all time, we know him best for discovering gravity (thus, the apple reference), but Isaac Newton did far more than that. His scientific discoveries revolutionized the world and ushered in a massive shift in perspective that had been building for a long time—a perspective which still permeates our thinking today. And this perspective is why the potentially life-changing event I'm about to highlight ended up being pushed aside in our mainstream thinking.

With the rise of "Newtonian Physics," the perception of the universe, which up to that point had fallen mostly under the domain of religion and philosophy, shifted into the hands of the scientific community. The next few-hundred years brought one exciting discovery after another, as science embraced the view of the world as a "machine" of sorts—a machine that operated within a basic cause-and-effect framework. The prevailing belief was that, through discovering the laws by which the universe operated, you would be able to determine, calculate, and predict everything. Over time, this foundational belief became accepted as fact. So, physicists and mathematicians focused on the *tangible*—what we could see, touch, and measure—while the *intangibles* were relegated either to the realm of religion or to the stuff of magic. That remains the predominant viewpoint still embraced by much of the world today.

There were tremendous upsides to the Newtonian focus on form, but there were also downsides. This focus caused anything *in*tangible and outside of the analytical, tangible world to be considered "taboo." The tangible was what intelligent, legitimate people focused on. This means that anything *in*tangible, other than what fell under the auspices of religion, was fodder for witch doctors and crazy people.

Over time, the intangibles became considered more and more "woo woo," and before long, the accepted view, not just in the scientific world but in most mainstream thinking, was: if something wasn't provable—if it couldn't be seen or touched—it was not to be taken seriously. It was too "out there"—too silly for smart, reasonable people.

And that was the prevailing thought for the three centuries that led up to the world-changing event we'll cover next.

— 4 —

The Foundation
of All Existence

By the time the early 1900s rolled around, Newtonian physics had reigned for almost 300 years, solidifying the belief that the world was physical and nothing more. By then, it had become clear that at the base of our world was one thing: *the atom.*

As a reminder of just how important the atom is, every single thing—both living and inanimate—is made up of atoms. It's the foundation of all that we see and experience from the time we wake up until we fall asleep. So, to be able to *split* the atom—to find out what is at the base of it—would reveal what is at the very core of everything, both human and otherwise. Knowing this would allow us to finally solve this ultimate mystery. Can you imagine? Without a doubt, it would be the most significant discovery of all time!

Because of this excitement, the early years after the turn of the twentieth century found many physicists across the globe working day and night to accomplish this feat: the splitting of the atom. While I'm sure scientific curiosity was mostly what fueled them, it probably didn't hurt to think of forever being known as "the" scientist or "the" group of physicists that was able to reveal the answer to this foundational question-of-all-time. The race was on, the pressure was intense, and these physicists were driven to discover the truth.

With that as a backdrop, let me ask you to answer this question as quickly as you can—off the top of your head (no Google searching or Siri support here): who *did* finally split the atom?

If you're like most people on the planet, you don't know. Think about it: splitting the atom is arguably the single most significant discovery of all time, and it unleashed the secret to the foundation of *all existence*—yet, we don't know off the top of our heads who did it.

Salk is famous for his polio vaccine. We know about Louis Pasteur's pasteurization. Einstein went down in history as having developed the theory of relativity. But no name rolls off your tongue about the discovery of the foundation of everything that exists? Such a significant finding, yet there's no clear "owner" of it—no one taking credit for it. Really?

I suspect the reason why lies in what was found when physicists *did* finally split the atom. After years and years of work and dedicated teams toiling around the clock, this is what was ultimately discovered at the core of all living and non-living things that you can see, touch, and experience:

Energy. Just … vibrating energy. In other words, nothing *tangible*.

All those brilliant, elite, Newtonian-trained scientists put their collective brains together and all they could find was energy.

Could it really be that at the base of everything tangible is something so *intangible*?

I can imagine the results became the proverbial elephant in the middle of the science lab. It must have shaken things up significantly, given that this discovery flew in the face of hundreds of years of accepted truth.

Perhaps the reason the successful, atom-splitting scientists didn't become household names is because no one knew what this discovery meant for humankind. After all, what should we do with the outcomes? How should we talk about this? We're still not sure today.

Releasing Outmoded Thinking

This fascinating chapter from history illustrates just how much we shun intangibles. After all, what do we do with the knowledge that energy is at the base of everything? How do we take charge of that? Since we don't know, we ignore it and keep looking at tangible things for solutions. Even this most important discovery of all time has been quietly placed on the back burner of history, not discussed in the mainstream of life, because the outcomes were not something you could touch, taste, or hold in your hand. The basis of everything we see and experience in life is *intangible,* but nobody's talking about it.

The truth is: life is rife with important intangibles. Pause right now to reach out and touch freedom, purpose, and love. Grasp a handful of joy. Bottle up peace of mind. You can't, and yet these are some of the most important drivers of our lives—the exact types of intangibles we strive for every day.

To illustrate how this tangible/intangible juxtaposition plays out in life, ask any parent on the planet this question: "What do you wish most for your child?" The response you'll likely hear is "happiness," yet another intangible.

But then, to help our children achieve that happiness, we frequently fall back on tangibles. We buy them nice clothes and the latest gadget, help them get into the best schools, hire tutors to help them get good grades, and so on—all in hopes of setting them up for a happy life. We revert to the tangible—what is outside of us—because we don't know what else to do. We know that intangibles matter, but we've never been taught how to harness them.

The bottom line is that happiness is not found outside of us. But we have a mistaken belief that it is, so we keep searching for that elusive external "something" that will finally bring us a joyful life. But when that search doesn't turn out as we had hoped and nothing seems to bring lasting happiness, we become increasingly frustrated. That's why we're living lives our ancestors would envy, yet 70% of the words we use to describe our modern world are negative.

This pattern repeats itself again and again because we are holding on to old ways of thinking. While those notions have served us well in the past few hundred years, they have also limited us.

We can't be hard on ourselves for believing that the key to the life we desire is found outside of ourselves. What else *would* we believe? Three hundred years of Newtonian physics taught us that *cause* is outside of us and that we are at its *effect*. Because we believe so heavily in this cause-and-effect relationship, it tends to leave us feeling victimized. After all, it's hard to feel any sense of satisfaction when we believe we are at the mercy of everything that is going on externally.

The solution to all of this lies in our ability to take charge and master the intangibles. But when most people hear that, their reaction is fear. I believe our fear of intangibles exists not only because intangibles are considered "taboo," but because they seem out of our control. We're so used to focusing on managing tangibles that we haven't thought much about the *in*tangibles. Even when we do think about them, we believe they are a byproduct of the tangibles, such as, "If I have enough money, I'll have a sense of freedom," or "When I have the right job title, I'll have success," or "If I get my kids into the right school, I'll ensure their happiness." So, intangibles have been widely considered "spin-offs" of tangibles.

Given that belief, we've never even considered how to take charge of the intangibles. We can, but we've simply forgotten how.

It's time to take the taboo out of intangibles and start recognizing the foundational and powerful role they play in how we lead our lives, day-in and day-out.

You are far more in control of the "un-seeable" than you may have ever believed. Through embracing the forgotten choice, you'll learn how to take back the reins of every aspect of your life and create for yourself those all-important intangibles. Much like Dorothy in *The Wizard of Oz*, who went searching far from home for something she already had within her, you're about to discover that you, too, have had—and still have—all that you need within you.

Let's begin by focusing on the intangibles that have the single-biggest impact on our lives: our thoughts and our beliefs.

— 5 —

The
What-You-Think-Is-What-You-Get
Pyramid

I don't believe the information I'm about to share with you is psychological, philosophical, spiritual, or religious. Its effectiveness doesn't depend on where you live, the culture you were raised in, your education level, or your socio-economic status. What you are about to read simply describes how a human being operates. As a result, it explains how our lives unfold every single day.

If we were born into this world with an owner's manual, the first three lines would say:

- What you **think** drives how you **feel**.

- How you **feel** drives how you **behave**.

- How you **behave** drives the **results** you get.

Take a moment to really reflect on these statements. Remembering this fundamental truth will help you get the most out of what I share in this book.

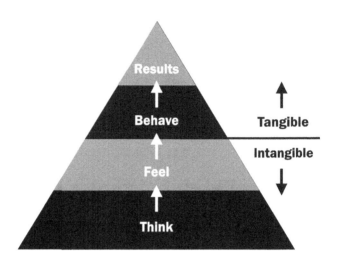

The What-You-Think-Is-What-You-Get Pyramid

The above diagram illustrates this flow, working from bottom to top, using thoughts and beliefs at the base. Let's see how this plays out in a real-life example.

Jordan, a talented executive coaching client, didn't feel great about his presentation skills. No matter how hard he prepared and how many times he practiced, when the time came to present, he muddled his words, sometimes drew a blank, and didn't deliver his message the way he had hoped. This was becoming more and more of an issue and was hampering his ability to move up the ladder in his corporate job. He had taken courses and read books on presenting, but nothing seemed to help.

I showed him this pyramid on a whiteboard, and we began to fill it in, starting at the bottom. "What's the key *thought* going through your head when you present?" I asked.

"I'm not that great at presenting," he replied.

"Okay, so as you start to present, if the underlying thought is, 'I'm not that great at presenting,' how does that make you feel?"

"I feel incompetent and self-conscious," he answered. "I'm nervous and lack confidence."

"So, Jordan, nobody knows what you're thinking or feeling—those bottom two steps are invisible to others. But what you think and feel drives your behaviors, and that's what others *do* see—what is tangible and visible to them. And if you're feeling incompetent and self-conscious, and you're nervous and lack confidence, how do you behave as you present? In other words, if I were watching you, how would I see you act, react, look, and sound?"

"You'd see me stumble over my words and lose my train of thought," Jordan replied.

"Got it. And since your behaviors drive your outcomes, what will stumbling over your words and losing your train of thought bring you? In other words, what results will you get from that?"

"I don't communicate what I want to say, so I end up confirming that I'm not good at presenting," he answered.

"Yes," I said. "This goes to show that *what you think is what you get.* The intangible thought or belief that you have about presenting works its way energetically through the pyramid and becomes reality."

The Think-Feel-Behave-Results Cycle

It's the same for all of us. The top two sections of the pyramid—the behaviors we display and the results we get—are tangibles and are all that anyone else can see and experience of us. But those tangibles are being driven by what we think and how those thoughts make us feel. So, behaviors and results are the *effects*—not the cause—of what happens in our lives. This is the way we all operate.

Using the pyramid model, here are examples of other challenges to demonstrate how this works—that what we think *is* what we get. In the pyramid diagram, the cycle progresses from bottom to top. But below, I've placed the four items in the order the cycle occurs, starting with what we think.

Think: "I don't make a good first impression."

Feel: When I meet someone new, I feel self-conscious, nervous, uncomfortable, stressed, and worried.

Behave: I become reserved. I hold back and don't speak much.

Results: I don't make a good first impression.

Think: "I never seem to have enough money."

Feel: When it comes to money matters, I feel anxious, fearful, limited, resentful, and jealous.

Behave: I don't buy things that I would enjoy; instead, I buy less enjoyable things simply because they are on sale. I talk about not having enough money, and I focus my mental energy on possible ways I might lose whatever money I do have.

Results: As soon as I build up a little extra cash, some expense always seems to come out of nowhere, so I never seem to have enough money.

Think: "I'll never find the right life partner."

Feel: I feel frustrated, helpless, jealous of other people's relationships, unattractive, and that I'm not good enough.

Behave: I never go out (there's no point). When I do meet someone new, I nitpick and look for what's wrong in anyone who shows interest. Then I withdraw and give up early.

Results: I never find the right life partner.

Think: "I don't think my work colleagues trust me."

Feel: When I'm around my colleagues, I feel unsafe, threatened, guarded, competitive, and insecure.

Behave: I don't talk much, I hold back, I don't share, I don't collaborate. When I need to get something done, I go behind their backs. I fall into passive/aggressive behavior.

Results: My work colleagues don't trust me.

This Think-Feel-Behave-Results process is universal. It applies to everyone on the planet, and it's happening within you right now. This pattern takes place beneath your conscious radar all day, every day, and is creating the outcomes you experience in your life.

It's self-fulfilling, too. Using Jordan's example, every time he thinks, "I'm really not that great at presenting," the outcome *confirms* his initial belief. Because what he thinks delivers the results he gets, the results he gets confirm what he thinks. Around and around it goes, further solidifying the thought until it becomes a well-entrenched, strongly held belief at the base of an ongoing vicious circle.

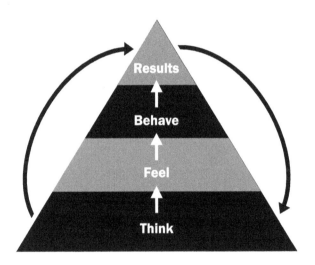

What you think drives the results you get, and the results you get confirm what you think, creating a vicious circle.

When you repeatedly think a negative thought or embrace a belief that doesn't serve you, it's like being on a hamster wheel that never goes anywhere but around. One of my clients labeled this "self-induced torture." I couldn't agree more.

The Proof: Your Own Life Experiences

Try this for yourself. Think of an area in your life where the results you're getting are far from what you would like them to be—the one area where making a shift would create the most improvement in your quality of life. Maybe it's related to your work, parenting, housing, family relationships, finances, health, or marriage. Once you've chosen the area where you want to focus, walk yourself through the What-You-Think-Is-What-You-Get Pyramid.

- Start at the bottom of the pyramid, and work in an upward direction.

- First, ask yourself the underlying belief you hold about that part of your life. What is the core thought/belief? Keep it as simple and direct as possible—one short sentence—and write it down.

  Here are a few examples:

    "I can't lose weight."

    "I don't work well on teams."

    "I'm not good at dating."

    "Teenagers are difficult."

    "My partner is lazy."

    "Making money requires hard work."

    "Men are _____."

"Women are _____ ."

"My family doesn't appreciate me."

"My boss doesn't like me."

"I'm really bad at small talk."

"I can't afford to live in this city."

- Once you're clear on the core thought/belief, ask yourself how thinking that thought or believing that belief makes you feel. Take your time to reflect on it, and jot down the feelings.

- Next, write down how those feelings cause you to behave. How do you act, react, look, or sound as a result?

- Once you are clear on those behaviors, ask yourself how they drive the outcomes you are getting.

Go back and look at the foundational thought or belief at the base of your pyramid, and compare that thought/belief to the results you get. Can you see that what you think really does drive what you get? The thoughts and beliefs you have related to that topic are responsible for your results.

For now, sit back and look at your completed pyramid. **If you apply this to every aspect of your life, you will see that you are literally shaping everything that happens to you through what you think and what you believe.**

People often say to me: "I'm doing well in my career, but I struggle with personal relationships," or "I'm a good parent, but my marriage is failing." Have you ever wondered why you can be so successful in one area of your life, yet those same skills don't seem to transfer to other areas? Use the What-You-Think-Is-What-You-Get Pyramid and notice how your thoughts and beliefs differ from one area to another. Walk each thought/belief through the pyramid model and see what you discover. If you're getting positive outcomes in some areas of your life but not in others, I assure you that if you look close enough, you'll discover—for good or for bad—your outcomes match your beliefs.

I've been using this model for many years with clients and for myself, and I still find it fascinating—and empowering. After all, who's in charge of your thoughts and beliefs? You are. So, the results you are getting in your life start from inside you. You are wholly responsible.

Conventional (Newtonian) thinking would have us see it differently. We would look at the top-two sections of the pyramid and believe that's where cause and effect play out—at the level of tangible behaviors and results. Thanks to the splitting of the atom, however, we are beginning to recognize that the true cause-and-effect relationship lies beneath the visible level, at the *intangible* level of thoughts and beliefs. And those thoughts and beliefs are what drive outcomes.

So, bottom line: cause is not outside of us, but inside. **Your thoughts are the cause; your life is the effect.** We experience what we believe, and recognizing this eye-opening truth is the first step to taking charge and getting different outcomes.

You are creating your life every single day through what you think and how you feel in reaction to what you think. You can choose to ignore this and continue to look outside of yourself for solutions. But every time you do that, you delay taking charge and creating the experiences you want.

If You're Not Sure About Your Thoughts/Beliefs ...

Identifying your thoughts and beliefs might be new for you, so if you find yourself struggling to pinpoint a specific belief or thought, try working backward within the pyramid model. You don't always have to start at the bottom and work your way up.

For example, maybe you are clear on how you *feel* about a situation, but you aren't sure about the thought/belief underneath that feeling. In that case, start at the feeling level of the pyramid. When you're crystal-clear about the related emotion, ask yourself, "What am I believing right now that leads me to feel like this?" Approaching the pyramid this way can help you identify the underlying belief.

Or maybe you're very clear on how you act or react, but you're not sure about the "under-the-radar" elements of feelings and thoughts. Start by writing down your behaviors and work backward to the feeling. Allow your natural curiosity to come into play. In what situations do you act this way? Why? What are you feeling? Thinking? Believing? Simply start wherever you are most clear and conscious, and allow yourself to be curious about the rest. You will eventually discover the underlying thought or belief.

Changing Behavior Isn't Enough

At first, some people find it challenging to accept that what they experience—their outcomes—originate from something as intangible as their thoughts. They make statements like, "But those are just thoughts. It's what I do or say that matters most, right?"

Case in point: A new client, Lina, and I were reviewing some written feedback she had received. After reading what her direct reports, colleagues, and boss had written about the behaviors she needed to improve, I asked if these inputs sounded similar to the feedback she had received in the past.

"Oh, yes," Lina said. "I've gotten the exact same feedback for three years in a row. No matter how much I try to do things differently, the feedback never changes."

I contacted a few of her work colleagues to find out more.

"I can see that Lina has really *tried* to make changes," they told me. "There are even long periods of time when her behavior is perfectly on point. But somehow, even when her behavior is what she wants it to be, it just doesn't feel 'real.' Something feels 'off.'"

That's not surprising. As a coach, I know that focusing only on trying to change behavior won't be sustainable because the beliefs and thoughts *beneath* those behaviors haven't changed. This also means that the feelings attached to the thoughts are still present.

So, just like Lina, even if you purposefully change your behavior, people won't buy it. It won't feel "real"—not to others and not to yourself. Remember: at the base of everything is energy, and that includes the energy behind thoughts and beliefs. Therefore,

any genuine and sustainable shift in behavior can only result from a foundational shift in what you think and believe.

Can you see how, if you just focus on changing your behavior without changing your thoughts or beliefs, you will get temporary results at best? That's what was happening with Lina as well. It wasn't until she changed her underlying beliefs that she finally received different feedback about her behaviors in the following year's review.

Perhaps this has happened to you, too—that no matter how much you keep trying to do things differently, you always end up with the same results.

Most of us have had the experience of starting a new job, getting into a new relationship, or beginning a health-improvement plan full of hope and determination that "this time it's going to be different." And for a while, it is. Yet, at some point, we find ourselves right back in that same familiar place, asking, "Why does this always happen to me? How did I end up back in this same situation?" or "How did I end up feeling this same way again?"

We tend to believe that we will get what we want through "doing" something. That taking some form of action—such as moving from job to job, from city to city, or from relationship to relationship—will be the catalyst for change. We focus on *behavior* because it's tangible, because we can see it and experience it, and because it's easier to monitor.

And since we've been taught to believe so strongly in the power of doing, we continue to *do* more and more, hoping that it will result in better outcomes. Yet despite all this nonstop doing, as indicated by the survey I mentioned earlier, we're a fairly unhappy bunch.

When we try to create a different outcome through "doing" alone, we don't experience sustainable outcomes because successful, long-term change doesn't take place at the behavioral level. But since that's where change first becomes noticeable, we mistakenly believe that's where it occurs. This explains why so many people feel that no matter how hard they try, nothing ever changes. **True, long-term, sustainable change first requires a shift at the intangible level of thought and belief. Then and only then will that shift drive a true change in behavior.**

We see this frequently in organizations. Companies large and small focus on implementing "codes of conduct" or "rules for behavior." After all, they are simple to regulate. When someone conforms to desired behavior, management can see it and call it out as "good." When someone doesn't conform, management can see it and call it out as "bad."

However, real behavioral change occurs in companies that implement what I call a **Unified Code of Beliefs**". What are the foundational *beliefs* that all employees or team members genuinely embrace that will drive the behaviors and lead to the results the organization wants to achieve? **Once those beliefs are aligned, that's how an organization or a team can achieve true, collective, and sustainable change.**

Through this pyramid exercise, I hope you can see how it is possible to take back your power *right now*. It really is under your control, as it always has been. But until now, the ability of your thoughts to create real outcomes may have seemed like some airy-fairy concept. That's because it was happening "under the radar," subconsciously. As soon as you become aware of this and raise those thoughts up out of the subconscious, pre-programmed mind into the consciously aware level, that's when everything starts to change.

— 6 —

The Rut of
Repetitive Thinking

The average human is estimated to have 50,000–60,000 thoughts per day (although I'm not sure who counted or how!) Can you guess what percentage of those thoughts change from one day to the next? Between 2-10%. That means roughly 90-98% of our thoughts are identical from day to day.

Imagine that—only a tiny fraction of the thoughts we have in any 24-hour period are different from one day to the next. This goes to show just how attached we are to our beliefs. And because we operate within the confines and limitations of consistent, ingrained thoughts and beliefs, it's no wonder we get the same outcomes over and over again.

Historian Will Durant summed up a portion of Aristotle's philosophy with this phrase: "We are what we repeatedly do." Based on that, it sounds like Aristotle may have been focused on the "outside"—on the behaviors he could see. Knowing what we know today, perhaps we should adjust this to read: "We are what we repeatedly *think and believe*."

What are the implications of thinking repetitive thoughts? We spend the bulk of our lives trying to solve problems, but we get frustrated because the same problems keep resurfacing. Can you see now that this is because we reinforce the same thoughts over and over without realizing it? So, of course, we continue to get the same outcomes.

To illustrate just how predictable we are, you're probably familiar with those online search-engine algorithms (called "behavioral" algorithms) that show you ads based on your previous internet searches. Even though they can be annoying at times, their accuracy is amazing. It just goes to show that our thought patterns are so programmed that a computer can easily predict what we are thinking.

The key to accessing more of your potential comes from examining your thoughts and beliefs. Just where did your predictable thought patterns come from? What are the sources of the beliefs at the base of your pyramid?

Reflect back on the one area of your life that you identified earlier—the area you would most like to improve and that you used as an example of how to work through the pyramid. Let's explore three potential ways to look at that belief. Do any of these three options apply to that specific belief of yours?

Option #1: Your belief is not true—and it never was

Just because you have a thought or belief doesn't necessarily mean it's true.

A colleague of mine named Rachel adhered to the belief "I can't lose weight." This was a decades-long, ingrained belief, and the longer she held onto it, the more "evidence" she gathered along the way to support it.

She began her first diet when she was just ten years old. She was hitting a chubby stage, and her mother, who also wanted to lose weight, thought it might be fun if they dieted together. The first week, they ate only "diet food," like steamed fish and string beans. At the end of the week, they had a weigh-in, and both showed a small loss. Over the next several weeks, they each continued to lose a small amount of weight by their Friday weigh-ins.

One day, after weeks of passing up foods she loved in favor of foods she hated, Rachel's weight stayed the same. Worse yet, her mother's weight *increased*. They both felt discouraged. It wasn't fair! Rachel's friends seemed to be able to eat whatever they wanted and were thin. Rachel, on the other hand, felt hungry most days and missed the foods she enjoyed. She felt like something was wrong with her. That afternoon, her mother took her out for a hot fudge sundae as a treat to commiserate their inability to lose weight. The next day, they restarted their diet. But when that week's weigh-in again failed to show a loss, they gave up.

Over the years, Rachel went on numerous diets and never expected much; she'd always lose a bit of weight but then stall out. Each experience served to confirm her belief that she couldn't lose weight.

Finally, Rachel joined a group of people who were losing weight, keeping weight off, feeling good, and taking care of themselves. What made this group different? They had completely different *beliefs* about health and wellbeing. They believed that they *could* lose weight, that their bodies were working with them, and that they were simply returning to a naturally healthy state.

This helped Rachel recognize that what was keeping her stuck was her ingrained thought that she couldn't lose weight. This decades-old belief had been driving her feelings and behaviors and had, in turn, created a self-fulfilling prophecy.

It wasn't really true that Rachel "couldn't lose weight." It was not her body holding her back—it was her beliefs. She was simply experiencing what she thought was true. Once she changed her beliefs, the weight started to drop.

As you look at your own beliefs, pause and ask: do you know them to be *true*? How do you know? It's an important question because, as you're now aware, those thoughts and beliefs are at the base of the What-You-Think-Is-What-You-Get Pyramid. That means they are the foundation of all you experience in life. So, understanding your beliefs—and making sure they are really true for you—is key.

To recognize this kind of false, limiting belief, look for phrases that start with words such as:

- *I'll never* … be fit, have enough money, find the right life partner, be good at writing …

- *I can't* … lose weight, speak up, have what I want, work fewer hours, change the system for the better, do what I love, dance, sing, find time to exercise …

- *I'm no good at* … relationships, technology, money management, public speaking, presenting my ideas …

- *I don't* … trust the system at work, think my boss likes me, feel like I have what it takes, know how to make my dream a reality …

- *I'm not*... tech savvy, good enough, smart enough, attractive enough, talented enough...

- *It isn't possible*... to ever be a charismatic leader, to reinvent my life at this age, to take a vacation due to my workload, for anyone to get ahead in this organization, for my mother and I ever to see eye-to-eye...

- *If I don't* _____, *then* _____ ... if I don't watch my back, they'll take advantage of me; if I don't do it, it won't get done right; if I don't say what they want to hear, they won't like me; if I don't finish everything on my list, I don't deserve a break...

Option #2: Your belief served you in the past but doesn't serve you now

Benjamin came to my office, upset and worried about potentially losing his job—something that had never concerned him before in his 20-year career. Though he had successfully built business for two decades, people were suddenly questioning Benjamin's ability to keep moving forward. The issue? He was viewed as a very poor leader.

Benjamin admitted he had never been great at leading others, but in the past that had been overlooked because he'd delivered such consistently outstanding business results. However, as he continued up the ladder at his company, his lack of people-leadership skills was having an ever-increasing negative impact on both his career and the business.

When Benjamin and I did his "leadership lifeline"—looking back at how he learned to be a leader of others, exploring the thoughts and beliefs around the subject—we discovered that Benjamin's first exposure to leadership in a work setting came from two years in the military, as part of his country's mandatory national service. The head of his platoon used a command-and-control, dictator style of leadership. So that became the model—the ingrained belief—for how Benjamin thought a leader should behave.

When he left the military and got into the corporate world, he naturally fell into using this same command-and-control style to lead his team. This worked for him for many years…until new, younger-generation team members showed up in the workplace. They had different expectations of how a leader should be. They didn't like Benjamin's dictatorial style and didn't respond well to being told what to do. As a result, Benjamin struggled to retain employees, and his reputation as a poor leader of others got increasingly worse.

He came to realize that his old, hard-wired belief that "a command-and-control form of leadership is best" was no longer working for him in the modern workplace. He had to let go of that and embrace a new belief that other styles of leadership would serve him better.

Another example: Growing up, Carlos had a mother who was prone to rage. If he expressed a feeling or opinion that his mother felt was in opposition to hers, she exploded with anger and withdrew from him. So for Carlos, being safe meant never speaking up or addressing any kind of conflict. Remaining quiet and going along with what others wanted had served him well, keeping his home life relatively calm in an otherwise volatile environment. This led Carlos to create the belief that expressing himself was dangerous because it would inevitably result in conflict.

So entrenched was this belief that, as Carlos got older, he integrated it into all aspects of his life, from his job, to his marriage, to his friendships. When something felt wrong or uncomfortable to him, he kept his mouth shut—avoiding any possibility of confrontation.

Over time, though, Carlos began to get push-back from others. His wife accused him of being cold and aloof. His boss grew frustrated with him, viewing him as lacking new ideas and not being invested in his work. Meanwhile, the friendships Carlos managed to maintain were lopsided, with his wants and needs never taken into consideration.

Of course, the people around him were completely unaware of Carlos's thoughts, beliefs, and feelings. All they could see and react to were his behaviors. Meanwhile, Carlos was confused and felt betrayed. After all, he was living according to his proven rule of "withdraw and be safe," which was supposed to keep him out of harm's way. But his behavior was no longer leading to positive outcomes.

By working through the What-You-Think-Is-What-You-Get Pyramid, Carlos began to see that his learned belief— "expressing myself is dangerous"—had served him at the early stages of his life, but it wasn't serving him anymore. In fact, in his adult life, it was producing the opposite effect from what was originally intended. By recognizing that the context of his life had changed, Carlos was able to differentiate the past from the present and shift this long-held belief. He started sharing his views and ideas more frequently, speaking up more when something bothered him, and pushing back when something didn't sit right with him.

What about you? What ingrained beliefs do you have today that might have been true in the past but aren't true now? If you are holding on to an old belief, consider: how is that belief still serving you? It must have served you at some point because you continue to hold on to it. But honestly, does it continue to serve you *now*? If a belief does nothing for you anymore—even if it's been around for years and years—you don't have to keep it.

Option #3: Your belief isn't really "yours"

Without realizing it, we sometimes adopt others' beliefs as true. Here's an example from my own past.

I was told by my second-grade teacher that I wasn't very good at drawing. She encouraged me to explore other avenues (like writing, which I guess in hindsight was a good thing). But because she had told me that, whenever I sat down to draw, I felt incapable and useless. And of course, because I didn't believe I could do it, what I drew was terrible, further confirming to my teacher and to myself that I really *was* bad at it.

Three decades later, a friend of mine, who is a talented, amazing artist, announced that she was going to teach an evening drawing class for beginners. "Would you like to attend?" she asked me. I chuckled, thanked her for the offer, and explained that I was the world's worst drawer.

She seemed determined. "I promise you—everyone can draw! I will show you how. In fact, here's my guarantee: if you're not able to draw by the end of the first class, you can stop attending, and I'll refund your money."

My friend believed in me, and I had nothing to lose. So I agreed to go.

Near the end of the first class, she came over to me, placed a shoe on top of the table where I was sitting, and said, "Here! This should be fun. Enjoy drawing this." Without a moment's pause —I didn't overthink it—I just gathered up what I had learned so far, dug in, and drew. Here's the result:

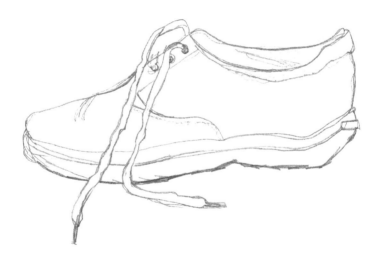

Is this a perfect drawing of a shoe? No. (And I'm definitely not giving up my day job anytime soon to become a fulltime artist.) But is it infinitely better than anything I had ever drawn up to that point? Absolutely.

I've kept this picture around as a reminder never again to accept someone else's belief in lack and limitation as my own.

The Beliefs We Inherit

When we adopt someone else's belief, it can be so subtle that we don't even notice it. Here are a few more examples.

A 52-year-old partner of an engineering firm walked into my office with very low energy. He had been in the same business for 30 years. On a scale from one to ten (ten being high), I asked him how passionate he was about his job. He answered, "Two."

"How long has it been like this?" I asked.

"For 30 years," he responded.

"So, how did you get into engineering in the first place?"

"When I was deciding what to study, my parents told me engineering was the best for me, and I followed their advice."

It wasn't his belief, yet he had held on to it for 30 years, resulting in a career that lacked passion.

Then, there's Derrick—a smart 38-year-old with lots of promise. But he was consistently plagued by money problems, never feeling he had enough. After I asked him to reflect on his underlying belief about money, Derrick realized he had one belief that was nagging and persistent: "The moment I see money in the bank," he told me, "I just know it's going to disappear."

A glimpse into Derrick's past revealed that his family was quite wealthy when he was young. From the time he was born until he turned 18 years old, his family had money. They belonged to private clubs and had nice cars and a nice house. Then, due to a couple of bad business deals, Derrick's father's career went off-track, and in a short time, they lost it all. His parents were forced to declare bankruptcy. This happened when Derrick was in his late teens—an impressionable period when he was learning how to handle money as an adult. Ever since, the belief that "money will always leave" was a daily, never-ending thought for him. He had inherited that belief from his father, but it didn't have to be true for Derrick, who was a young, capable adult with a different life situation.

As a final example, I'm reminded of a story a friend shared with me. A woman was getting ready to cook a ham for a holiday celebration—an annual tradition her family had embraced since her childhood. As always, to prepare it for the oven, she cut off the ends of the ham equally on the left and right sides.

"I've seen you cut off the ends of the ham every year," her husband said to her. "I'm curious—what's that about?"

"That's how you cook a ham," the wife answered.

"No, really," the husband pushed back. "What's the reason for cutting off the edges?"

"This is how my mother cooked ham. It's just the way it's done."

At the husband's insistence, the wife called her mother to ask the reason.

"Oh, my dear," her mother chuckled, "my roasting pan was always too small for the hams your father brought home, so I simply had to cut off the ends in order for them to fit."

Reflect honestly: where did *your* beliefs come from? Parents? Society? School? Teachers? Key influencers? Television? Videos? Bosses or ex-bosses? Are your beliefs really "yours," or are they someone else's that you adopted as your own? Have you simply picked them up unexamined and downloaded them before questioning whether they would serve you or match the life you want for yourself?

As the examples from all three options demonstrate, beliefs are often playing out in our lives without even knowing they're there, let alone that they are driving outcomes. They're dictating our lives because they are running around unchecked.

To uncover these false thoughts, I encourage you to pause when you discover a belief and say it out loud—hear yourself say it. Or have someone else state that belief back to you. Once you hear it outside of yourself, it's likely you'll realize it isn't true. At the very least, stating your belief out loud gives you the opportunity to look at it more closely. *Is* it true? Was it true once, but no longer fits? Is it someone else's belief but not yours?

If you find yourself wanting to understand where a belief came from, remember this: it doesn't matter *where* the belief came from or *why* you developed it. You may also find that some beliefs are harder to let go of than others. None of that matters. What matters most is to ask yourself these questions: Is this belief serving you now? Is it driving the outcomes you desire?

Of course, it's entirely up to you if you want to keep thinking what you've always thought and believing what you've always believed. It isn't unusual for people to cling to their thoughts and beliefs as if they were a security blanket. Indeed, we can be very quick to dig in and fight for beliefs—in some cases, even be willing to go to war for them, as though our very lives depend on preserving and maintaining those beliefs.

Holding on to old beliefs is an option you will always have. But before you do, it's important to examine *why* you hold on to them.

The Need to Be Right

Here's the interesting thing about beliefs: we have a deep-seated need to be right—to prove a belief that we have embraced is "correct." So we find a way to reinforce our beliefs no matter how much hurt or pain they cause us. In a later chapter, we'll talk about why we have this tendency.

In the meantime, here are a few personal and professional examples of just how strongly we feel the need to prove our beliefs:

- You believe your father never listens to you. So to prove yourself right, you focus on the times when he doesn't listen and ignore the times when he does.

- You believe your family thinks you're a lousy cook, so you criticize your own dinners every night. Eventually, someone agrees with you that the main dish is a little dry, confirming your belief. You discount any compliments and look at food left on your family's plates as proof that they hate your cooking.

- You believe you aren't doing enough to be a good parent, so you talk about and focus on every soccer game you miss because you have to work late. You discount all the special moments you spend with your kids and the stable life you provide for them.

- You believe you are 100% right about a big disagreement you had, so you choose to hold onto "your side"—causing you angst, irritation, and frustration—rather than choosing to find common ground, which would bring you peace.

- You believe that Joe from Operations is always late to meetings, so every time Joe *is* late, you pay close attention to that, reinforcing your belief. When Joe does show up on time, you dismiss it as "a fluke."

- You believe that Joanne isn't good at writing, so every time Joanne hands you something written, you read the document looking for evidence to confirm your belief. When Joanne *does* turn in a well-written document, you assume someone must have helped her.

- You believe you can't make money doing what you love, so you spend your life in well-paying jobs that you don't like or enjoy. If, by chance, you happen to find yourself in a good-paying job that you *do* love, your foundational belief is so strongly ingrained that you sabotage it and get fired, once again proving yourself right. You do this even at the expense of the potential for long-term happiness in your career.

If you see this kind of habit occurring, the fundamental question to ask yourself is:

Would you rather be *right* or *happy?*

Would you rather be proven correct or be in a place of joy? Start watching…you'll likely be astonished at how many times you choose to be right over being happy, just to confirm that your beliefs are correct.

The Forgotten Choice

Hopefully, you now see why your thoughts and beliefs are such critical intangibles and that they have the single biggest impact on the outcomes you get. They are the foundation of everything you experience—or don't experience. If you aren't 100% happy with your day-to-day existence—if you want to shift to a better job, career, marriage, relationship, financial status, or even better health—you will need to change the thoughts and beliefs that serve as the foundation of it all.

To do this, we need to return to the outcome of splitting the atom and the importance of what was found at its base: energy.

Why? Because just as energy is the essence of all matter, energy is at the core of every thought and belief. There are two types of energy that form two foundational thought-systems, and we are subconsciously and constantly choosing between these two systems. This is the most critical choice we can make, day-in and day-out: the forgotten choice.

— 7 —

Which Energetic State
Will You Choose?

Picture this: You're heading home at the end of a long day, weary and tired. You stop by a convenience store to buy some bread, and while you're at the cash register, you notice that the latest lottery tickets are for sale. The payout is $150 million dollars, so on a whim, you decide to purchase a ticket. You gather your bread and lottery ticket, get back in your car, and drive to your house. After dinner, still feeling exhausted, you decide to check the news before going to bed. The numbers of the winning lottery ticket are being revealed, one-by-one, in the bottom right corner of the screen. As you watch the numbers unfold, you suddenly realize you have the winning ticket. You've just won a fortune!

How would you react? Given the common belief that money means freedom, you would probably shift from feeling tired to feeling thrilled, excited, and exhilarated. You would likely jump up and down, hug your spouse, grab your children, and dance around the room.

What does this demonstrate? That we can choose which energy to embrace at any moment. Even though you felt tired and weary, your belief about winning the lottery gave you a sense of possibility. And the energy of that belief in possibility completely shifted your experience.

This energetic choice holds true for all thoughts and beliefs. That's because *energy comes in two distinctly different states* that fuel two separate thought-systems: One that is destructive and based on *fear*, and the other that is constructive and based on the *Joy of Possibility*.

Every moment of every day, you have the ability to choose between these two distinct thought-systems. And since thoughts serve as the foundation of the What-You-Think-Is-What-You-Get Pyramid, the choice you make between those two states is wholly responsible for how your life unfolds.

You don't have to believe me. You'll experience this yourself as we go along.

A Tale of Two Thought-Systems

To get a sense of how these different energetic thought-systems function, imagine your mind as having two communication channels that play all day and all night. Both channels address the same subjects—career, relationships, parenting, health, finance, science, technology, lifestyle, world events, environment, human interest, travel, hobbies, entertainment, and so on. Nothing is left out. But these two channels are programmed to present these subjects in completely different ways. They represent totally different foundational mindsets.

One channel sounds like this: *Protect your portfolio! Is your child falling behind? Be on alert for this latest virus! How to avoid getting fired! Prepare for the coming global crisis! Everyday household items that could be killing you! Slow down aging! Why relationships fail, and how to protect yours!*

The other channel addresses the same subjects but sounds like this: *Grow your portfolio! Fun ways to inspire your child in math and science! Six tips for self-care! Create healthy habits! How to ensure your next promotion! Thriving in today's economy! How to build stronger relationships! Day trips that will leave you feeling inspired!*

At first glance, you may say to yourself, "But isn't this just thinking positively versus thinking negatively?"

No, this is far subtler than basic positive-versus-negative thinking. I'm talking about **two separate energetic states of being.** And the choice you make to embrace one or the other has the potential to either lead you in the direction of your dreams or far away from them. Positive thinking alone is not powerful enough to do that. Your energetic state goes much deeper.

These two thought-system channels are available 24/7/365, and when you tune into one, the other becomes unavailable. You can surf back and forth between them, but when you're listening to one channel, it isn't possible to hear the other. Most of us surf back and forth continually between the two and end up living in a state of static—which looks and feels like stagnation.

Our thoughts, which are at the base of the pyramid model, work just like the two separate channels I described. They either align with fear or with the Joy of Possibility. The thought-system we choose informs and affects our feelings, drives our behavior, and produces our outcomes.

The ability to consciously choose the Joy of Possibility over fear is the essence of the forgotten choice. Since this choice is so critical to our outcomes, let's dive deeper into each of these two thought-systems.

Thought-System #1: Fear

Ah, fear. We're so familiar with it. Yet if I ask you, "Are you a fearful person?" based on my experience asking this question of thousands of people around the globe, you would likely respond with a knee-jerk, "Nope. Absolutely not. Fearful? Not me!"

We don't think of ourselves as fearful. Stressed? Yes. Frustrated and angry? Sure. But fearful? No.

And yet ...

Fear permeates our world. Fear of failure. Fear of success. Fear of missing out on social media. Fear of being too involved in social media. Fear of commitment. Fear of lack of commitment. Fear of intimacy. Fear of loneliness. Fear of crowds. Fear of being silent. Fear of speaking up. People-pleasing out of fear of being disliked. Bullying out of fear of being vulnerable. Fear that we won't stand out. Fear that we *will* stand out. Fear of not getting a promotion at work. Fear of actually getting that promotion at work. Fear of being too big. Fear of being too small. Fear of war. Fear of crime. Fear of sickness. Fear of people who are different. There's an endless list of fears that we regularly experience.

An interesting aspect of fear is that it runs deeper than we might have imagined. Feelings such as anger, jealousy, envy, rage, scarcity, and worry are all fear-based.

If you find it hard to believe that fear is at the foundation of an emotion like anger, you're not alone. Just recently, while listening to a friend describe in great detail how angry he was about a certain situation, I asked him what fear might be at the base of his anger. His response was immediate and guttural: "I am *not* afraid! I'm just angry."

It's not an uncommon response. The truth is, we are often in denial about experiencing fear because it makes us feel vulnerable. Given the options, most of us would rather show anger than demonstrate any signs of vulnerability. So, whatever fear is driving the anger slips under our radar. But if you dig deep enough into anger, you *will* find fear. Which one? Well, there's a full menu of options.

You get cut off in traffic and feel angry. What is underlying that anger? Fear of almost being in an accident, fear of being injured or killed, fear of your car being damaged, fear of your car insurance premium going up, fear that your rights don't matter, fear of conflict, fear of being treated badly by the other driver, fear of being incorrectly blamed for a potential accident ... That's just to name a few.

Think of the parent who explodes in anger when their young child runs out into the street or when their teenager comes home way past curfew. At face value, you could say that the parent is angry at the child's behavior. But look more closely. In those situations, anger most likely resulted from a fear that the child could be hurt in some way. Even if a parent insisted that the anger was not based on concern but was related to being "disrespected," well, guess what? That still goes back to fear. Maybe it's a fear of losing authority or a fear that without respect, their children will become liars, addicts, never get jobs, and wind up on the streets. The fear-based mindset can be quite the drama queen.

Don't get me wrong—there's absolutely nothing wrong with wanting to prevent your children from running into traffic! It's perfectly natural to want your child to honor a curfew that you set and to call to let you know they're going to be late. And there's nothing wrong with feeling angry if they don't. The point I'm making here is that, if you dig deep, you will see that beneath the anger—beneath any anger—there is always fear.

So, once again, even though we don't think of ourselves as fearful people, I guarantee that if you really dig deep and look at the source of your anger, you'll realize that some (often unidentified) fear lurks beneath it. The same is true of all other negative emotions such as judgment, irritation, disgust, frustration, sadness, grief, and a sense of lack. Name any negative feeling, and I promise you that fear is the energy underneath it.

As I mentioned, fear is one of two foundational energetic states/ mindsets that are at the base of all thoughts and beliefs. But how did that come to be? Are we fearful by design?

Life's Classroom: Learning to Fear

We are not born with fear. In fact, I believe babies exist in a complete absence of fear, which is why we love to be around them so much. They are happy, joyful, carefree, fully relaxed, and completely trusting.

Instead, fear is *learned,* over time, and we learn fear *through* fear. "Stop fidgeting—you look ridiculous." "Don't talk to the neighbors because they're not like us." "Do this, or else …" And that "or else" may mean being punished in some way, such as not getting dessert or gifts, not being able to invite friends over, or not getting into the right school. Later in life, it can mean not getting the job we want, not marrying the right person, and on and on.

Mind you: we are taught fear with a positive intention—to keep us safe. But eventually, there is so much fear-based learning that it becomes a main driver for us. We may think of some fears as "natural," like the fear of falling or the fear of heights, but those aren't *learned* fears. Instead, they are part of our inborn guidance system—our *intuition*—that protects us from physical risks.

Just to be clear, I'm not blaming parents here. In no way do I want to contribute to any "my parents did me wrong!" narrative. We all simply teach what we believe, and we believe in fear because it's what we were taught by those who came before us.

The fears that each of us were taught vary to some degree. They reflect our culture, our parents or guardians, where we lived, who we grew up with, and what was happening in the world at that time. We might have been taught to fear people from different countries, people with different-colored skin, people who believe in different ideologies, and so on. Our fears may be very personal, such as the fear of dogs, squirrels, clowns, balloons, or flying. Some fears may be shared, like the fear of the unknown, of being hurt, of punishment, failure, pain, or loss.

As we grow, so does our belief in fear. We begin to fear being ourselves, making mistakes, not fitting in, and being rejected. Over time, everything we do—how we work, communicate, eat, exercise, live, and love—becomes tinged by some level of fear.

So even though fear is not our natural state of being, like anything that's practiced over and over, fear-based thinking becomes our default system.

I estimate that by the time we're in our late teens or early adulthood, we are operating primarily from our fear-based thought-system. By then, we've become one big walking bag of under-the-radar thoughts and beliefs, the majority of which are based on fear.

Like a hamster on a wheel, this pattern continues throughout our day-to-day existence. We routinely run on fear without consciously realizing it. Indeed, fear is so prevalent in our lives that we've trained ourselves through years of repetition to justify it as a strong *motivator*. We eventually come to believe that fear is *necessary* for us to achieve what we want in life, to succeed, to contribute to society, to be good parents, to be promoted, and so forth.

Case in point: Not that long ago, I attended a professional speaker's convention. One of the individuals presenting focused his entire speech on fear, sharing phrases like: "Embrace your biggest fear!" "Let fear be your guide!" "Fear is your greatest friend!" We so believe in fear that we even idolize it.

Our beliefs about fear can be confusing. On the one hand, you maintain the belief that fear is necessary—that it motivates you and drives your success. But think about it: how can you possibly live up to your full potential if you're always operating from a state of fear? You can't. And on some level, you already know that.

That's why, on the other hand, you're aware that fear limits potential, so you'd like to be seen as fear*less*. If someone asks if you are afraid, your first reaction will likely be, "No!" Why?

Because deep inside, you recognize just how much fear really does limit you.

Which brings me to a question that I get asked frequently: *Can* fear be motivating? My response: absolutely. But fear will only ever motivate you *away* from something you *don't* want. Fear will never motivate you *toward* the experiences you *do* want.

Start observing yourself. When you're facing a challenge—a shift in career, difficulty with a relationship, a disagreement at work, a tough conversation, feeling hurt by something someone has said, or worrying about a conflict—pause and ask yourself: what energetic thought-system underlies that? I guarantee that a fear-based belief is there, lurking at the foundation.

The Stealth Nature of Fear

I don't need to teach you about fear. You already know it. But I *do* want to point out some aspects of fear, given its stealth nature and how accustomed we've become to letting it run our lives unchecked.

Most of the time, fear doesn't show up on the surface *looking* like fear at all. That's what makes it so hard to identify. Here are just a few of the less obvious ways fear masquerades itself.

People-pleasing: People-pleasing may look like an effort to make everyone happy, but if you look more closely, at its root are fears of disapproval, punishment, and/or abandonment. We try to please others, whether it serves us or not, out of fear of losing them.

Positive thinking: "Think positively!" cry certain gurus. But positive thinking can often be a mask intended to protect us from the fear of vulnerability or from addressing other underlying fears. When this happens, it's akin to throwing glitter over your fears and hoping that no one notices, least of all yourself.

Little white lies: We all tell little white lies once in a while. The key is to look at what is underneath them. Fear of coming across as unkind or hurting someone's feelings? Fear of rejection if we give an honest answer?

I'm not saying little white lies aren't occasionally justified, but what is ironic about them is that they are not only based on fear—they actually perpetuate it. For example, if *you* tell little white lies, that means *others* are doing it, too, so you begin to doubt that people are telling you the truth.

I'm not trying to stop you from ever telling a little white lie. My aim is to encourage you to take a closer look at what drives the decision to lie in the first place, as well as to recognize the energetic state that your decision is aligned with, knowing the outcome it will produce.

Protecting those you love: Let's say that you're concerned your home might be broken into, so you decide to take measures to protect yourself and your family. You add a few heavy-duty locks to your front door, you have bars installed on your windows, and you buy a weapon.

At first, all this added protection keeps you feeling nice and safe. But before you know it, the fear starts to creep back in. Every time you lock or unlock the door, look at the bars on the windows, or clean your weapon, you start to feel a little uneasy. You're reminded why you took all those actions in the first place. I mean, what kind of world are we living in that needs so many locks, barred windows, and weapons?

So, you do what any fear-based thinker does, and you increase your protection even more, adding security cameras around your property, and getting a trained German Shepherd. Yet, before long, the fear starts to creep back in again.

When you are operating from the fear-based thought-system, there will never be enough locks, window bars, barking dogs, or weapons to quiet the fear that there is something to be protected *against*.

To see how this plays out, just look to some of history's well-known dictators, and note how they became increasingly paranoid with each new level of protection. Case in point: by the end of World War II, Hitler was living in a bunker located about eight-and-a-half meters (28 feet) underground. It was reinforced by four meters (13 feet) of concrete and had a concrete roof that was three meters (nearly 10 feet) thick. Despite all of that protection, Hitler still wouldn't take a bite of food without having someone else taste it first to make sure it wasn't poisoned. Even when we have so much protection available to us, fear is reinforced.

As you can see, fear doesn't always manifest itself in ways we expect. Having looked closely, though, we can see how each behavior in these examples *is* based in fear. We are always trying to find ways to solve the problem of fear—we get angry, people-please, lie—in hopes that, by doing so, the fear will be resolved.

These are the ways that a thought-system steeped in fear tries to fix issues. When you look at it that way and see it for what it is, it's fairly innocent. Sad? Maybe. Ineffective? You bet. But ultimately, it's just innocent.

More importantly, it will never work. Because the more we behave in these ways, the more fear is reinforced. The more white lies we tell, the more we think everyone else is lying, too. The angrier we get, the more it reinforces anger. The more protection we install, the more it fuels our need for safety. In the end, all of this just solidifies the very fear that we hoped to escape in the first place.

But once we realize this, it's *empowering*, too. When we are armed with the knowledge that it's only a fear-based mindset that causes us to shift into judging, deceiving, and yelling, the emotions lose their heaviness—both in reaction to the fear within ourselves and the fear within others.

Of course, the point is not to become *afraid* of fear. That's the last thing you need—more fear! No, fear-based thinking isn't some dastardly evil. It's simply ineffective in delivering the outcomes we desire. Fear-based thinking is actually "avoidance thinking." Every time we are hurt, either physically or emotionally, we do everything we can to avoid having that experience again, not only for ourselves but for other people, too (children, direct reports at work, friends, and so on). This is how fear-based thinking gets passed down in the first place. We can easily become preoccupied with helping others avoid making the same mistakes we've made or that we've witnessed others make in the past.

The point here is to be able to see fear for what it really is and to recognize when you are operating on autopilot, choosing fear out of preconditioning. Then, look closer and get crystal-clear as to what fear is costing you.

The Cost of Fear

Even though fear has become the foundation of so much of our lives, fear will never lead us correctly. The fear-based thought-system thrives on lack, and from that position, we are incapable of making good decisions that serve us well.

Fear always creates more fear. Just like dogs produce puppies, and cats produce kittens (dogs and cats could never produce alligators or ostriches), fear can only ever produce more fear.

When you're stuck in fear, you cannot experience the feeling of satisfaction that comes from living up to your highest potential. At best, when in fear …

- You can get the career promotion you hoped for, but you'll work endless hours for fear of losing it.

- You can meet the life partner of your dreams, but you'll worry constantly that they'll leave you for someone else.

- You can finally lose that extra weight and get in shape, only to find yourself anxious around food and afraid you'll gain the weight back if you miss even one of your workouts.

- You can finally achieve a previously unfathomable financial goal only to find yourself still thinking, "It's not enough."

- You might even become an Olympic athlete, but when you get there, fear will barely subside long enough to let you enjoy one moment of the experience.

You may have heard the phrase, "No problem can be solved from the same level of consciousness that created it." I agree. Fear is an energetic thought-system, and *from within that system, there is no way out.*

When we're in fear, we wall ourselves off. We hold back, hide, pretend, defend, judge, and lash out in anger. The simplest of events can trigger us to obsess. An eye roll, a "look," or some offhanded comment can send us into a tailspin.

Fear keeps us from showing up. It costs us our health, happiness, and the ability to create, dream, live, and just relax and have fun. It keeps us from living our purpose. It can deaden our relationships and steal every possibility of joy from our lives.

Ultimately, that's the cost of fear. And it's one hell of a price to pay.

Why We Hold on to Fear (Instead of Drop-Kicking It)

Have you had enough of fear yet? Me, too. But if we hold on to fear and continuously choose it, it must mean that we honor it. Otherwise, why in the world don't we just let it go?

The answer is simple and obvious: We *believe* in fear. Here's an example to illustrate that.

My husband, Daniel, and I lived in Thailand for 11 years and enjoyed exploring the various regions of such a wonderful country. One weekend we decided to visit up north, where a tour guide took us to an elephant camp whose proceeds are focused on supporting the survival of this magnificent species.

What I remember most about that trip was this: walking around the camp, I witnessed a mother elephant and her baby chained to the ground—each with the same-sized stake. The mother elephant weighed in at 2,700 kgs (almost 6,000 pounds), so it was very clear to me that she could have easily pulled on her chain and yanked that feeble stake out of the ground. In fact, given her mammoth size, she could have done that as effortlessly as I could remove a candle from a birthday cake.

When I asked the chief elephant wrangler about this, he explained that baby elephants are trained to stay in place by having a chain wrapped around their ankle and fastened to the ground by a stake, providing them only a small area in which to move around. At that age, the chain and stake are enough to hold them in place.

What makes this so fascinating is that, even though the chain and stake become no match for fully grown elephants, the elephants don't know this. They have been taught to believe that the stake and chain will keep them in the exact same space, so they stop trying. It isn't a chain that keeps them staked to the ground, it's simply a thought—a learned belief in limitation.

When we take fear as our guide, we are living much like those elephants, in a limited thought-system, cut off from what we are truly capable of being and doing. Through years of conditioning, we have come to accept these limitations as the truth, leaving us essentially staked to the ground by nothing but the flimsy chain of our fearful beliefs from the past.

Because these thoughts of lack and limitation seem so normal, it's a very rare person who isn't living some version of a "staked-to-the-ground" life. As mentioned before, our first impulse is to deny that we're operating out of fear. We're stressed, that's all. Overwhelmed. Tired. Irritated. Overworked. Angry. But we're not fearful ... right?

Then, once we recognize that we *have* been running on fear, we tend to defend it, saying that it's justified, well-founded, and even helpful. Most of us have never been willing to look at fear and question it or, better yet, to see what might happen if we chose a different option.

This constant fear-based state of upset feels unavoidable because most of us spend a large part of our day in that state. Despite our desire for a stress-free existence, someone or something always seems to mess it up. Your boss makes you furious, your employee screws up, or breaking news has you feeling panicky. You get cut off in traffic, miss an important call, and despite your new diet and hitting the gym all week, you somehow manage to gain weight.

Every day, hundreds of little and not-so-little things seem to derail our best efforts to live the life we want. This eventually leaves us frustrated, overwhelmed, and quite frankly, pissed off— all feelings that are based on what? Yep, fear.

If you remember one thing about fear, remember this: even though fear has become habitual to us—constantly running as our default system—*it is not our natural state*. We weren't born with fear. Instead, we've trained ourselves so well in fear-based thinking that we don't even realize anymore how truly *un*natural it is. Nor do we recognize how much fear has become the mental scaffolding of our modern-day world.

Here's a surprising truth: all fear is based on the past. Perhaps that seems hard to believe given that a lot of what we worry about is based on the future. Examples: "What if I won't have enough money to retire?" "What if I get sick?" "What if I lose my job?" But those "future fears" reflect beliefs that we've either developed or were taught in the past. We fear loss and limitation because we have been *taught* loss and limitation. That's why fear holds us back from moving forward toward the joyful existence we want.

Much has been written about fear—how to overcome it, fight it, live with it, or face it full on. But as you know by now, I see it differently. **Fear is simply a choice we make, so it is completely within our control. And we can choose differently.**

This is what I think makes the forgotten choice so transformative: once you become aware of just how much of your life you've spent operating within the fear-based thought-system—when you recognize the limiting effect it has had on you and the outcomes you've experienced—you will also realize it isn't serving you and that there is an infinitely better choice you can make. Once you start consistently making that different choice, you'll notice big changes in both your personal and professional life.

We have spent tremendous time and energy keeping the fear-based thought-system intact. Isn't it time we apply just as much effort toward letting it go?

Thought-System #2: The Joy of Possibility

If fear is energetic Thought-System #1, then what energy fuels the second thought-system? In other words, what is the opposite of fear?

My client, Jacob, and I were reviewing fear-based thoughts at the base of his What-You-Think-Is-What-You-Get Pyramid. After getting clear on which fear was driving a particular outcome he was getting at work, I asked Jacob what he thought the opposite of fear would be. He looked at me, perplexed, so I clarified,

"Instead of running *away* from fear, Jacob, what could you be running *toward?*"

He thought for a while longer, then responded, "I don't understand. After all, I don't want to be running 'toward' fear, right?"

In Jacob's mind, all options included fear. This goes to show just how steeped we are in the fear-based thought-system. We're so neck-deep in it that we sometimes can't even imagine that a non-fear-related option exists.

But there *is* another energetic thought-system—the opposite of fear—that can lead you toward being your best self and living up to your highest potential. As alluded to earlier, I call it the *Joy of Possibility.*

Why that name? Because this energetic thought-system is… well… full of *joy*, and it's experienced as a complete absence of fear. It's through this energetic state of joy that what was previously just potential now becomes possible.

Pause and recall a Joy of Possibility moment (or "JOP" as I call it, pronounced "jawp")—a time when you felt limitless. When you were truly happy, open, enthusiastic, seeing the world as full of potential and without limits. What moment comes to mind for you? For me, it was the first time I rode a bicycle without training wheels, and I experienced the sense of freedom that the whole world could be explored on that bike. I also felt that strong sense of JOP the first time I flew overseas and also when I graduated from business school with several job opportunities available.

Maybe the moment you recall was a long time ago, or maybe it was recent. Either way, anchor yourself in that moment and keep it in mind. By doing so, you will remember the feeling of JOP, which will help you align with that energetic state more easily going forward. You can use that memory as a way of dialing back into that state.

When you align with the Joy of Possibility, there is a profound sense of potential. It's characterized by openness, limitlessness, clarity, fun, curiosity, creativity, and wholeness. While in this state, you continually experience a feeling of "what could be," yet there is also a very in-the-moment trust in both yourself and others.

The Joy of Possibility is about freedom to relax and be present, to be yourself because you're not worried about judgment. You experience it when you're singing in the car or in the shower, belting out a tune without worrying that someone will hear you.

When you operate within this energetic thought-system, you experience a sense of balance, peacefulness, release from control, and a calm, inner self-confidence. JOP is a state of *being*, not a state of doing.

If this sounds alien to you, let me assure you it's not. The Joy of Possibility is in everything that grows in nature—animals, trees, plants. When something impedes their way, they simply work or grow around it, moving forward with natural instinct, not fear.

As children, we were the same. If you place a crawling baby on a floor that has a plate-glass circle in the middle, under which there is a significant drop in height, once the baby reaches that glassed area and sees the drop, the baby won't crawl over the glass. But the baby doesn't recoil in terror either (as an adult might). The baby simply pauses, lets natural intuition kick in, and switches course to crawl around the glass to get where it's going.

So, JOP was natural to us as infants and toddlers. We just need to remember it. We've simply fallen out of practice due to the prevalence of fear in our lives.

The Joy of Possibility in Action

To illustrate what I mean by the Joy of Possibility, if you weren't lucky enough to witness figure skater Sarah Hughes perform in the 2002 Olympics, do yourself a favor and watch it on YouTube. Her performance was pure JOP in action.

As with most Olympic Games, that year's women's ice-skating competition was fierce. By the halfway mark in the performances, sixteen-year-old Sarah found herself in fourth place. Statistically, there was very little probability of her winning. As she stepped onto the ice to perform in the finals, she was in a position from which no one had ever gone on to win the gold.

But in possibly the biggest upset in Olympic figure-skating history, Hughes did win the gold, going from fourth place to first place in four-and-a-half breathtaking minutes. It was a perfect demonstration of what can happen when you are operating in the Joy of Possibility.

Hughes later said, "I didn't think I had a chance of winning a medal, much less the gold. So I didn't even think that. I skated because I love to skate. I just let everything go." She was skating for the pure joy of it—with possibility—not driven by the fear of losing. When you are in a state of JOP, there can be no fear. So you're able to let go and not get derailed by self-doubt.

While it's true that Sarah Hughes trained for years leading up to her show-stopping performance, the beauty of JOP is that it can be experienced by anyone, novice or professional, and at any time.

In fact, you probably know the term "beginner's luck," where you try something new for the first time and do it perfectly, only to find that you fail miserably the second or third time. Maybe you've experienced this yourself—you bowled a strike on your very first try, hit the perfect tee shot during your first time on a golf course, or nailed that complicated yoga position on your first attempt.

I believe that what we call "beginner's luck" is actually the Joy of Possibility in action. When we try something for the first time, we're in a state of openness and curiosity. Our mind is not yet filled with all the rules or any of the limiting beliefs about how difficult the task might be.

Here's another example: Ashok, a coaching client who was looking to change jobs, hadn't interviewed for a long time, so he decided to "practice" with three similar jobs that he wasn't particularly interested in. He came back amazed, interview after interview, reporting that he had sailed through the discussions and was offered a job all three times. Why? There was no fear involved in these discussions, so he approached the interviews with openness, curiosity, and nothing to lose.

The Joy of Possibility energetic thought-system feels good, like being wholly centered, because it's our *natural* state—the state in which we were born. This is why, when people begin to re-experience JOP, they often refer to it as a feeling of "returning home." **It's through accessing this state that we step in, fully embody, and take back what we're capable of being and doing.**

When clients or audiences hear me talk about JOP, one of the most frequently asked questions is: "How can I learn the Joy of Possibility?" The beauty of it is: you can't. You already have all the JOP you'll ever need. It's that "something more powerful" that you've had since birth. **It's innate—it's who you are when you strip away the learned, fear-based thought-system.**

Living in this state doesn't come from taking on new behaviors, but through letting go of the fear-based thoughts and beliefs that don't serve you. **The Joy of Possibility doesn't have to be learned—it just needs to be** *remembered.*

JOP is also what we refer to as being "in the zone." Just like Sarah Hughes, professional athletes, dancers, and artists demonstrate this state of being when they are tuned in and fully present. Perhaps you recall a time when you, too, were in the zone. When did you feel the most free, emboldened, capable, switched on? What was that like? What brought it on? Recalling that—and re-experiencing the energy you felt at that time—can help you as you remember and realign with the Joy of Possibility.

What might you do if you could reclaim your natural, unlimited state? Imagine yourself completely free from fear. Who would you be if you weren't afraid? Afraid of making a mistake. Afraid of being judged. Afraid of failing. Afraid of losing it all. Afraid of taking a risk.

If you've been hanging out in fear long enough, you might find yourself wondering just how JOP has the power to change anything. So, let's clear something up: in no way is JOP the wimpy, small, or limiting mindset that fear would have you believe. It isn't a fantasy state that only a select few can achieve, where everything is all sunshine and rainbows. It's quite the opposite. The Joy of Possibility state is how you were before you were taught fear. It is how you can live now if you consistently remember the forgotten choice.

This may seem foreign to you right now, and its intangible nature can make it hard to describe. But you know the Joy of Possibility when you see it, you know it when you feel it, and you know when you're around it.

Case in point: as I mentioned, babies are always in a state of JOP, which is why we love being around them so much. But I suspect you've also encountered certain adults who operate within this energetic state. Perhaps it's a leader at work who inspires you or an amazing artist you admire. Maybe it's that free-spirited business mogul for whom everything just seems to work out beyond most people's wildest dreams.

These are the people who just seem switched-on, happy, and quietly powerful. If you've ever wondered what's behind that, wonder no longer. They are simply tapped into and living in JOP, and it's that energy that makes them truly magnetic.

When you encounter someone operating within the Joy of Possibility, you'll likely sense it immediately, often even before you see evidence. These individuals can be found in every walk of life, and the characteristics that differentiate them from each other are as varied as their personalities. But what is the same—and what makes them so powerful—is that they are completely and utterly aligned with JOP. They're always growing, creating, and curious about "what could be."

A Brief Recap

The answer to achieving what you want in your career, relationships, finances, or anything else in life lies in learning to take control of your thoughts and beliefs. However, we woefully underestimate their power, primarily because they are intangible, and to this day, we're still not taught to take intangibles very seriously.

At the base of the most important intangibles—your thoughts and beliefs—is either one energetic state or the other: fear or the Joy of Possibility. The thought-system you decide to embrace is fueling the most important choice you can make at any point in time—the forgotten choice. Once we strip away the darkness of the fear-based thought-system, we discover a better, brighter choice lies underneath, based on possibility.

— 8 —

Two Energies, Two Pyramids

We've already seen how the What-You-Think-Is-What-You-Get Pyramid model works. Now that we know there are two energetic thought-systems, let's look at how the foundational thoughts and beliefs at the base of the pyramid operate when founded either on fear or on the Joy of Possibility.

Remember my client, Jordan, who had issues when delivering presentations? His belief ("I'm not that great at presenting") resulted in outcomes that matched that belief—visible behaviors that confirmed to him and others that he *wasn't* good at presenting. As a reminder, here is Jordan's original What-You-Think-Is-What-You-Get Pyramid process:

Think: "I'm not that great at presenting."

Feel: I feel incompetent and self-conscious. I'm nervous, and I lack confidence.

75

Behave: I stumble over my words, and I lose my train of thought.

Results: I don't communicate what I want to say and end up confirming that I'm not good at presenting.

With this as a background, I explained to Jordan the two thought-systems—fear and the Joy of Possibility—and asked him which of those he felt was at the base of the pyramid we had just reviewed.

"Fear, without a doubt," he responded.

"Reading back over this pyramid, Jordan, to what extent is this fear-based belief serving you?" I asked.

"Serving me? I can't see any benefit, so I don't think it's serving me at all."

"How open are you to changing this and putting this behind you once and for all?"

"Completely open," he replied.

"Great," I said. "Since you agree that the outcomes you are currently getting stem from a fear-based belief, what different belief—founded in the Joy of Possibility—could you embrace that would lead to a different outcome?"

He paused for a while before responding. "Well, the obvious choice is to say something like, 'I'm a great presenter,' but honestly, that just doesn't work for me. It's too far from the truth."

Nodding, I said, "I understand—that just sounds like positive thinking, so it won't be sustainable. What about the belief 'I'm *learning* to be a great presenter'? Would that be a statement you could embrace? Is that true for you?"

"Yes, I like that! That definitely works for me."

"When you've been in the process of learning something," I shared, "say, for example, how to ride a bike when you were a child, you've fallen down on occasion, right?" He nodded. "But that didn't stop you from getting back on the bike. When you're learning something, you give yourself permission to fail because, after all, you're simply learning. That means you aren't an expert yet, so that gives you some leeway."

With Jordan's new belief—"I am learning to be a great presenter" —as the foundation, he created a new What-You-Think-Is-What-You-Get Pyramid, based on the Joy of Possibility. His new belief read like this:

Think: "I am learning to be a great presenter."

Feel: When I present, I feel open, comfortable, more relaxed, more confident.

Behave: My body language is stronger, and I speak more naturally. I engage more with people when I'm presenting.

Results: I learn to be a great presenter.

That dramatic shift in outcomes stemmed from one thing and one thing only: a shift in thought.

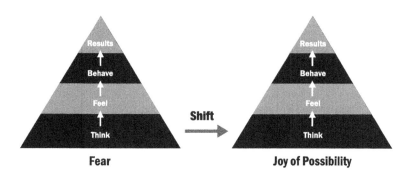

Use the What-You-Think-Is-What-You-Get Pyramid to achieve different outcomes through shifting from fear to the Joy of Possibility.

If you've found yourself wondering, "Could the answer to all of the challenges I face be as simple as shifting the way I think?" I hope you realize now that the answer is "yes." It may seem hard to believe that exchanging an old belief for a new one can have that kind of effect. But after working on this with thousands of people, I can assure you it can and it does. Indeed, it cannot *not* work—it's simply the way we operate as humans.

Some people say, "But it's so hard to change my ingrained beliefs!" That may seem true, but what is even harder is operating in a fear-based thought-system, day-in and day-out, in a way that doesn't have you jumping out of bed ready to enjoy amazing experiences. *That's* what's truly difficult.

What I'm advocating is not so much that you immediately choose to embrace a new thought or belief, but that, as a start, you begin to question old beliefs. Begin to notice what you're thinking, and ask yourself, "Is it really true? How might my life be different if I thought about this in a new way?" Simply recognizing the link between your thoughts and your outcomes is a powerful shift in and of itself.

Your Very Own What-You-Think-Is-What-You-Get Pyramid

I hope by now you can see that through this pyramid exercise, you can begin to take back your power—immediately. It's 100% within your control, as it has always been. **Because your thoughts are the cause, and everything else is simply effect.**

Until now, the power of your thoughts to create real outcomes may have seemed like a foolish concept. That's because it was happening under the radar. However, as soon as you become aware of this and raise those thoughts up out of your preprogrammed, subconscious mind into your conscious awareness, everything starts to change.

I've been working with this What-You-Think-Is-What-You-Get Pyramid for many years, yet it never ceases to excite me. Why does it enthrall me so? Well, first of all, who's in charge of your beliefs? You are, of course, so you can change them. It's also exciting because, if you're like many of my clients, this may be the first time in your life that you review the thoughts and beliefs that are driving your existence and consciously choose new ones to create different outcomes.

If your thoughts and beliefs aren't delivering the results you want, then just like Jordan—who initially believed he couldn't present well—you, too, can use the pyramid model to shift. This is how you upgrade those outdated thoughts to embrace new beliefs that will deliver what you desire.

We're going to shift consciously from a fear-based belief to a JOP-based belief and use the What-You-Think-Is-What-You-Get Pyramid to do so. Let's look back on the fear-based pyramid examples from before and see how the outcomes change based simply on shifting the underlying belief.

Original, Fear-Based Pyramid

Think: "I don't make a good first impression."

Feel: When I meet someone new, I feel self-conscious, nervous, uncomfortable, stressed, and worried.

Behave: I become reserved. I hold back and don't speak much.

Results: I don't make a good first impression.

New, JOP-Based Pyramid

Think: "Making a great first impression means focusing on others more than myself."

Feel: When I meet someone new, I feel curious, interested, calm, comfortable, and confident.

Behave: I place my attention on them and ask good questions to get others to open up.

Results: I make a great first impression.

Original, Fear-Based Pyramid

Think: "I never seem to have enough money."

Feel: When it comes to money matters, I feel anxious, fearful, limited, resentful, and jealous.

Behave: I don't buy things that I would enjoy; instead, I buy less enjoyable things simply because they are on sale. I talk about not having enough money, and I focus my mental energy on possible ways I might lose whatever money I do have.

Results: As soon as I build up a little extra cash, some expense always seems to come out of nowhere, so I never seem to have enough money.

New, JOP-Based Pyramid

Think: "I trust that I will meet my financial goals."

Feel: When it comes to money matters, I feel calm, relaxed, and optimistic about the future and the possibility of financial growth.

Behave: I notice what it feels like when I *do* have money. I talk about my finances from a positive point of view. I budget for and buy things I enjoy. I look for ways to increase my income, as well as ways to grow the money I have.

Results: I meet my financial goals.

Original, Fear-Based Pyramid

Think: "I'll never find the right life partner."

Feel: I feel frustrated, helpless, jealous of other people's relationships, unattractive, and that I'm not good enough.

Behave: I never go out (there's no point). When I do meet someone new, I nitpick and look for what's wrong in anyone who shows interest. Then I withdraw and give up early.

Results: I never find the right life partner.

New, JOP-Based Pyramid

Think: "The perfect partner will come to me when the time is right."

Feel: I feel hopeful, open, comfortable in myself, trusting, assured, and excited about the possibility.

Behave: I get out more often. I try new things. I'm curious about the new people I meet, and I engage them and ask questions. I relax and am myself.

Results: The perfect partner comes to me at the right time.

Original, Fear-Based Pyramid

Think: "I don't think my work colleagues trust me."

Feel: When I'm around my colleagues, I feel unsafe, threatened, guarded, competitive, and insecure.

Behave: I don't talk much, I hold back, I don't share, I don't collaborate. When I need to get something done, I go behind their backs. I fall into passive/aggressive behavior.

Results: My work colleagues don't trust me.

New, JOP-Based Pyramid

Think: "My colleagues and I are all aiming toward the same successful outcome."

Feel: When I'm around my colleagues, I have a sense of camaraderie. I feel supported, comfortable, and safe.

Behave: I'm relaxed and open. I share, I collaborate, and I'm direct and upfront when there's an issue that needs to be resolved. I focus on the future and what can be.

Results: Both the company and I experience successful outcomes, and my colleagues trust me.

Now, let's apply this to you. Think back to the area of your life you previously identified where the results you are currently getting are far from what you would like them to be.

As you review your original, fear-based thought/belief, look at it from a new perspective, this time with the Joy of Possibility at its base. Have some fun with this! Try going through the pyramid with a completely opposing belief. How would the opposite thought or belief make you feel? How would you likely behave if you felt those feelings? How would you envision the outcome? Continue to play with it. How might entertaining these different thoughts produce different outcomes for you? How might your life experiences change now that you recognize the power to drive the outcomes you want lies in your ability to consciously choose your thoughts and beliefs?

For this exercise, be sure to choose a thought based on the Joy of Possibility that works for where you are in your life right now. If you can shift immediately to the complete opposite of your fear-based thought—in other words, moving from "I am *not* great at _____" to "I *am* great at _____," then go for it. If, like Jordan, you are not yet sold on believing that new thought, try the approach of "I am *learning* to …" In my experience, this latter approach works best for most people because when learning to do anything new, there is a joy in that. The process of learning places us in a state of curiosity and possibility. "I am learning to be a great leader," "I am learning to be a good parent," "I am learning to manage money successfully." The important thing is that you're able to embrace the new thought right now, and feel it as real. Eventually, you'll be able to move toward the opposite of that original thought: "I *am* great at …"

Once you recognize that you can shift out of fear-based thinking, you can start to take control of your life by making the conscious decision for the Joy of Possibility. This forgotten choice is open to you at any point in time.

Working from within the Pyramid

If you're unsure of what a new belief rooted in the Joy of Possibility might sound like, there are several ways you can approach it. In my earlier example with Jordan, we worked directly from the *base* of the pyramid—changing the foundational thought. But that isn't your only option. There are other ways you can work within the pyramid to create a new belief that will work for you.

For example, start with the results you would like to achieve. Keeping those outcomes in mind, here are a few ways to work within the pyramid and clarify the foundational JOP-based belief that will help you achieve what you want. Ask yourself:

- … what **thoughts and beliefs** would support those outcomes? Sometimes, it's helpful to think about it like this: if someone else were trying to create these outcomes, what thoughts and beliefs would that person embrace?

- … what **feelings** would help you to experience those results? By being clear about the feelings that would best create what you want, you can choose a new thought that supports those feelings.

- … what **behaviors** would support your desired outcomes? Once you're clear on that, you can work backwards. What feelings would drive those behaviors? What new thought could you choose that would bring about those feelings?

Remember: you can't simply change your behavior and get the results you want. In order to create different outcomes, your behaviors must match your thoughts and beliefs. The way you act, react, look, and sound all need to be consistent. This is what I call being "vertically aligned." There are no shortcuts.

Changing a behavior without changing its related underlying belief will never work. That's why two people can "do" the exact same thing and get entirely different results—because the feelings and beliefs at the base of those behaviors are different from person to person.

Can you see how identifying a fear-based thought, then *consciously deciding* to change it to a JOP-based thought will result in a completely different outcome? This is the essence of the forgotten choice. It is a simple yet transformational shift, and now that you have learned how this works, you can start to take control of your life at any time by consistently making the choice to embrace the Joy of Possibility.

Success is based on becoming acutely aware of your thoughts and beliefs and regularly asking yourself: "Which thought-system is at the base of what I'm thinking and believing right now? Are my thoughts based in fear or founded in the Joy of Possibility?"

This is how we create, all of the time. To be aware of that is the greatest reminder ever. We've simply forgotten that this choice exists, which is why consistently bringing this choice to our conscious awareness—and choosing purposefully for JOP—is so life-changing. Because when we are energetically aligned to the Joy of Possibility, we are *unlimited*. By contrast, when we take fear as our guide, we will always be as limited as we think we are.

Fear or JOP—It's Either One or the Other

Very little in life is truly black and white—most of life is lived in the gray. But there is one critical exception: when you are in the fear-based thought-system, you cannot be in the Joy of Possibility. And when you are in the energetic state of JOP, you cannot be in fear. The decision for one or the other is binary. It's either/or, black or white, fear or JOP.

I recall speaking with a client about a situation she was facing at work—a conflict with a colleague. After she explained the details of their problems and how it was making her feel, I shared the What-You-Think-Is-What-You-Get Pyramid with her. I showed how the base aligns with either one or the other of the two foundational energetic thought-systems. Then I asked her which of the systems she believed was at the base of this particular work relationship: fear or the Joy of Possibility.

She paused for a moment, then responded, "A bit of both."

Based on my experience, most of us feel the same way. We tend to believe that we are able to blend the two systems. But, in actuality, that isn't possible. If you really watch your mind, you will see that you are either in the Joy of Possibility or you are in fear. It can feel like "a bit of both" because we often shift back and forth quickly between the two. But it's impossible to be in both energetic states at the same time. There can be no fear, not even a drop, when you are in the Joy of Possibility—and vice versa.

That's because the two thought-systems are completely separate and mutually exclusive. At any moment, you are allowing either one or the other to be in charge.

How can you tell if you're in fear or JOP? Just asking that question sounds crazy—you'd think it would be crystal clear. But it takes focused attention—at first, anyway—to notice which channel you are tuned into at any given time.

Here are some suggestions for how to tell whether you're tuned into fear or JOP:

- Do you feel a sense of restriction and limitation or a sense of expansion?

- Do you feel anxiety or certainty?

- Do you feel weighed down or lighthearted?

- Do you feel dread or excitement?

- Do you feel judgment or curiosity?

- Do you feel a desire to control, or do you feel open and flexible?

It's very clear-cut: if you are feeling even the slightest sense of unease, of not being centered, of not being at peace or happy, you are in fear. There is no other option.

Realizing the energetic state you are in relies on paying attention to the most important conversations you have every day. Let's explore.

— 9 —

Your Most
Important Conversations

Take a moment right now and reflect on the most important conversation you've had in the past week. Maybe you spoke with your daughter regarding her report card results, or perhaps you had a meeting with your boss about an important project. Maybe you chatted with your spouse about retirement plans. Of all the conversations you had this week, which one would you say was the single-most important?

If you respond that your most critical conversation was with another person, I think you're mistaken. I believe the single most important person you speak to every day is not *outside* of you—it *is* you.

We talk to ourselves nonstop from morning until night, day-in and day-out. It's as natural as breathing and eating, but we are often unaware of it. If you see a child playing alone, a person staring into space at a bus stop, or someone sitting quietly at their work desk, I promise you they are each having a mental conversation.

And those inner discussions—which you normally don't even realize you're having—contain the single most important words you hear on any given day. In fact, more than any other conversation you have, your internal dialogue is indicative of the outcomes you'll experience. That's because **your self-talk is continuously, yet unknowingly, reflecting and reinforcing your existing thoughts and beliefs.**

If you're feeling fed-up, beat-up, or just plain frustrated with the results you're getting in any aspect of your life, your self-talk is likely driving that. **Self-talk is foundational to your belief in who you are and what you can achieve.** It impacts every area of your life and can build you up or tear you down. It influences how you communicate and connect with others. It reflects and reinforces your self-confidence and your self-concept. It can be your best friend or your worst enemy.

If you don't like something that's happening in your life, listen to your mental chatter. Notice what you're saying to yourself about that topic, and you will get a clear indication of what's driving the results you're experiencing.

Start to pay close attention to your inner conversations. Listen carefully … for one day, three days, or a week. Take note of what you hear.

- Does your self-talk start the minute you wake up, or do you allow your mind to rest before it begins?

- Is what you say to yourself helpful, understanding, supportive, exciting, creative, and focused on growth? Or are your words about plotting, planning, judging, defending, defeat, anger, or blame?

- Does the energy of your self-talk shift according to the subject matter?

- Which energetic thought-system would you say your self-talk is most often aligned with: fear or the Joy of Possibility?

- Based on the self-talk you hear most frequently, would you regularly seek out the counsel of this voice?

The World's Worst Boss

Pauline walked into my coaching office with her head hung low and slumped into a chair with a groan. "You aren't going to believe this one, Brenda," she said. "What a colossal mistake I've made!"

She then proceeded to share her distress with me in detail: a project plan gone wrong, missed deadlines, an upset client, relationships damaged, team demoralized…and Pauline's self-trust at a new low, too.

"I can't believe I did that," she lamented. "What's wrong with me? I'm such an idiot! Sometimes I question if I even know what I'm doing."

"Wait a minute," I responded, holding up my hand to give Pauline a moment to collect herself. "Let me repeat back to you what you just said. 'I can't believe you did that, Pauline! What's wrong with you? You're such an idiot! Sometimes I wonder if you even know what you're doing!'"

I paused while Pauline registered the impact of hearing her own words spoken back to her. Then, I asked, "Pauline, I'm curious…

if your boss spoke to you that way, would you continue to work for that person?"

"No, absolutely not," she answered without a moment's hesitation. "I would never put up with that kind of language."

"But," I pointed out, "those are the exact words you just said to yourself."

As author Seth Godin puts it, self-talk is often the "world's worst boss," regularly making nasty comments and often without our being aware of it.

When Pauline heard her own words repeated back to her, she discovered two key takeaways:

- First, she realized she was harder on herself than she would ever be on others, and that she would never allow others to be that hard on *her* either. Yet she tolerated it—regularly— without realizing it. (Does that sound familiar to you?)

- Second, she began to see how counterproductive her negative self-talk was. It served no other purpose than to keep her in a fear-based thought pattern. And the stress related to that fear would likely end up causing her to make even more mistakes, sending her into a downward spiral.

Can you see now why self-talk is indeed the most important conversation you have?

Self-Talk—Your Number One Informant

Perhaps you've spent years in the dark, unaware of the thoughts and beliefs hidden below the surface that have been driving the results of your life. All of that can change easily if you spend some time listening to your self-talk.

It won't take long before you'll notice patterns in how you speak to yourself. You'll hear what your self-talk believes about money, relationships, your job, your children, and so on. Just listen. You'll suddenly realize that your self-talk couldn't keep quiet if it tried. It will reveal your beliefs, one after the other after the other. That's why I call self-talk "Your Number One Informant." It's always been talking. Now that you are aware of the importance of self-talk, you can begin to listen deliberately.

Your self-talk holds the key to your subconscious—those intangible, below-the-radar beliefs that are most likely keeping you aligned with the energetic thought-system of fear, filled with lack and limitation. When I mention to clients that these beliefs are usually subconscious, they often say, "That's bad news, right, since those types of beliefs can't be changed? The fact that they are 'under the radar' makes them inaccessible, correct?"

No, the only reason these subconscious beliefs run so much of our lives is because they haven't been brought to our conscious awareness. These habitual beliefs started long ago and became solidified. Over time, we've become completely unaware of them, so we don't recognize their ability to drive the outcomes of our day-to-day experiences. They've just become the norm, and we don't think of them any other way.

Of course, you know now that you *do* have a choice. This choice comes from watching your thoughts very closely and bringing your subconscious beliefs to your conscious awareness. That's when you can change them, and that's when life not only becomes incredibly fascinating, but downright fun.

Bottom line: if you are not happy with your current situation, change your self-talk. Become a master of your inner speech. **After all, you are *both* parties in those inner dialogues—both the speaker and the listener—so the entire conversation is within your control.**

Referring back to the two-pyramid What-You-Think-Is-What-You-Get model, we know that our foundational thoughts and beliefs are driven either by fear or the Joy of Possibility. To represent those two energetic states of being, **your self-talk has two distinct voices that speak to you all day long: the *Inner Defeatist* (the voice of fear), and the *Inner Coach* (the voice for the Joy of Possibility).**

The Voice of Fear: The Inner Defeatist

Since the Inner Defeatist is the voice of our fear-based thought-system, it views everything through the lens of threat, lack, limitation, and scarcity. Fixated on the idea of loss, the Inner Defeatist obsesses over everything it believes went wrong in the past, what is going wrong in the present, and what could go wrong in the future.

This fixation on what's "wrong" can leave you continually looking for someone to blame. The fear-based mindset *loves* the idea of blame. When you're listening to the Inner Defeatist, *who* is to blame doesn't really matter, whether you blame yourself or someone else. What matters is maintaining the belief in fear, and nothing maintains fear better than blame.

When you first hear the word "Inner Defeatist," perhaps the image that comes to mind is someone who is constantly beating you down, leaving you insecure, scared, and struggling. It's the voice that regularly points out how you've messed up. However, this description of the Inner Defeatist is only part of the story.

That same voice also produces thoughts of arrogance, bragging, bullying, and obsession with winning. It's the voice that talks about how *others* screwed up—pointing out that your boss is a narcissist, your coworker is a jerk, your teenager is spoiled, and your next-door neighbors are bringing down the neighborhood. That's because the Inner Defeatist is divisive and maintains fear through the concept of winners and losers, victims and villains.

So, the Inner Defeatist can come across in two very different ways of speaking, but it's ultimately the same voice—continually seeking to perpetuate blame.

I want to make one point perfectly clear: **The Inner Defeatist isn't "bad." It simply reflects a learned view of the world that isn't natural and that doesn't serve us.** The challenge with the Inner Defeatist is that it often talks first and loudest, so it's bound to be attention-grabbing. In fact, the Inner Defeatist is dramatic and enjoys exaggerating and wallowing in problems. It operates by being loud, interrupting, and adding more fuel to the fire whenever possible.

You can choose to listen to and believe the Inner Defeatist—or not. There is another, better choice.

The Voice for the Joy of Possibility: The Inner Coach

Well-known American basketball coach, John Wooden, once said, "A good coach can change a game. A great coach can change a life." Of course, you know that no one but you can truly change your life, but I love this quote anyway. After all, wouldn't you like to have a great coach by your side, someone who is focused solely on your wellbeing and continuously offering support and guidance all along the way?

What you might not realize is that every one of us has nonstop access to an amazing coach just like this. We are born with it. Think of it as your full-time, "built-in GPS."

I call this the Inner Coach, and when you are operating in the Joy of Possibility thought-system, this is the voice you hear. The Inner Coach operates from a place of complete trust, speaking with assurance and calm confidence. We are all born with full access to the Inner Coach, which is why small children are so open and uninhibited (at least until they're trained to ignore and override the Inner Coach).

You may not have had the words to describe it, but you have no doubt experienced the Inner Coach at some point. Perhaps you thought of it as intuition, a gut feeling, or an intangible sense of just "knowing" something—a hunch or a nudge.

In today's fast-paced modern world, the more technology we have, the less likely we are to tune in to the Inner Coach. We get distracted. It isn't that technology itself disconnects us from our Inner Coach; it's that we hand over our power to gadgets, to our smartphones, to the next shiny thing, with little if any conscious awareness of what we're doing. Is it any wonder then that, in both subtle and not-so-subtle ways, we've been learning since childhood to shut out this incredibly helpful resource?

Today more than ever, we find ourselves living in a constant state of busy, busy, busy. The fear-based part of the mind *loves* busy! Since busy-ness is often steeped in fear, it blocks the Inner Coach. Adding to that, we also block the Inner Coach with distractions such as food, alcohol, drugs, sex, binge-watching television shows, and constantly obsessing over our fear-based thoughts.

If this sounds familiar to you, here's some good news: though you can (and likely often do) ignore the Inner Coach, you can never lose your connection to it.

The Inner Coach is a constant—it hasn't changed since the minute you were born, and it never will. It has always been running 24/7/365, and it's on call at a moment's notice. It knows you, even when you've been "offline" and hanging out in fear for a long time. Even when you're feeling angry, frustrated, hopeless, and defensive. Even when you've lost track of what you are capable of and have forgotten that you have another choice, your Inner Coach is still there, patiently ready and waiting for you to choose differently.

The Inner Coach guides you in many ways, and over time, you may find that guidance uniquely personal to you. For instance, let's say you suddenly notice yourself humming a song you haven't heard in years. For some reason, the lyrics keep playing over and over in your mind. You go to bed singing the tune, and you wake up hearing it in your head.

If you are like most people when this happens, you find yourself wondering how in the world you're going to stop the "lyric loop" that's driving you crazy—it's so annoying! Instead, what you could do is pause and consider the possibility that those lyrics might not be random at all. The words may actually provide some form of support or a message from your Inner Coach.

This guidance comes all day long... that nudge you feel to step out and grab a coffee. The article that shows up on your phone. Perhaps a chance encounter with someone in an elevator that leads to meeting just the right person to help get your latest project off the ground. Once you start checking it out, you'll be pleasantly surprised—and frequently blown away—by just how well this inner GPS is guiding you every step of the way. But you will never know it's there if you ignore the promptings.

The Inner Coach: A Personal Journey

These promptings occur for both small matters and big life changes. You don't always recognize it when you're experiencing it, but when you look back on the past, what may have seemed like chaos full of jagged edges can be seen as a smooth and perfectly straight line. Here's one of my own personal examples.

I was working for a wonderful company in the U.S. and was engaged to be married to a man who lived in a different city. Maintaining our long-distance relationship was proving to be tricky, so my fiancé and I made a pact: we would both apply for overseas positions in our respective corporations and, as soon as one of us was offered an expat job, the other would follow. Very excited at the prospect of starting our lives together as expats, we let our companies know we were interested in working overseas.

A few weeks after that, early one Monday morning, I was called to my boss's office. "Good news, Brenda—you're moving to Prague!" she said with a smile.

I bought and read every book I could find about the Czech Republic. What a gorgeous city Prague was! Everything I read pointed to it as the best travel destination in Central and Eastern Europe. I was thrilled!

The *following* Monday morning, though, my boss gave me different news. "Sorry, Brenda, there's been a change of plans. You're moving to Warsaw, Poland instead."

Now, no offense to Warsaw, but from the photos I had seen, it definitely didn't look like Prague. The sudden and unexpected switch felt like an enormous blow.

To add to the drama, based on phone calls with my fiancé, he suddenly seemed to be anything but excited about the whole "moving overseas" thing. Every time we chatted about Warsaw and our potential move, I could sense his reticence. In fact, he kept finding reasons to postpone our look-see visit to Poland, where we would experience Warsaw, have a chance to view places to live, and get a sense of what life would be like there. He first postponed the trip by two weeks, and then another two weeks, and then another and another, until three months had passed. My company was justifiably losing patience.

My fiancé finally committed to a date for our look-see visit, and the plane tickets were purchased. I was to meet him in New York City, and we would fly to Warsaw together. At 11:30 p.m. the night before I was to catch my early morning flight to meet him, I was all packed and just getting ready for bed when he called to say that he had decided not to go on the trip.

Too late to back out, I had no choice but to go on the look-see visit by myself. Given that my fiancé and I were supposed to be on this trip together, the company had appropriately arranged a "couples' visit"—setting up several activities, all with other couples. So, to add insult to injury, I attended an entire week of couples' events *by myself.*

At the end of the trip, I flew back to New York City to meet my fiancé for lunch and to share the exciting details of my look-see trip, what Warsaw was like, what job possibilities there might be for him, and so on. I was hoping my newfound enthusiasm for the city would shake him loose from whatever apprehension he was experiencing about our relocation. But as soon as I stopped talking, he looked me in the eye and said, "I will not follow my woman around the world."

His words shook me to the core. Through that one short sentence, not only did I learn that my fiancé was not going to move overseas with me, but I also realized that he wasn't the person I thought he was. This was not the relationship I knew I wanted.

With that, I took a deep breath and called off the engagement.

I then had another decision to make: should I still move to Warsaw, or should I stay in the U.S.? My family warned me not to go. My friends warned me not to go. A river of fear-based thoughts also ran through my head: "Don't go! If you do, you'll never again have a chance at a happy personal life!"

But there was an even stronger (yet quieter) voice inside that spoke with a surprisingly calm sense of confidence. "Go," it said. And somehow, I knew it was the right thing to do.

So, "go" I did, moving to Poland in the cold of late winter where the sun only shown a few hours per day. Perhaps it was the lack of sunlight that helped usher in my own personal dark night of the soul, which began soon after I arrived. I found myself completely alone in a foreign country where people communicated in a language I didn't speak, in true hardship conditions, and in a new job with a new team that was at least twelve weeks behind due to the repeated postponement of my look-see visit. To get around, I had to learn to drive a stick-shift car in the snow (I had absolutely no idea how). And the extraordinarily high cost of long-distance phone calls from Poland back then meant that any connection to family—my lifeline of support—was kept to the bare minimum. I had been warned that it would be hard, but I had no idea *how* hard. Add to that the grief I was experiencing from the loss of my personal relationship, and the whole experience seemed like a living nightmare.

I threw myself into my work, hoping to numb the pain of what had happened. But no matter how hard I tried, every night before going to sleep, nothing prevented me from hearing the final words of my former fiancé: "I will not follow my woman around the world."

During that first year in Poland, it was so easy to focus on everything that was going "wrong"—my broken engagement, the hardship conditions, and the fact that this was certainly not anything I had imagined my life abroad would be like. Yet, here and there, I began to find myself having moments of joy—joy of learning a new language, of making new friends, of discovering just how resilient I was. I felt excitement as my team and I grew the company's brands and I developed as a leader.

For months, I seemed to vacillate between what I now know to be fear and the Joy of Possibility. But with every day that I focused on "what could be," I started to sense that maybe I was right where I needed to be. What I had once believed to be hardship and chaos felt more and more like opportunity.

Now, when I look back on that period of my life, I can't help but smile. The decision to move to Warsaw was one of the best choices I've ever made. I lived there just a few years after the Berlin Wall had fallen, so Poland quickly became the powerhouse nucleus of Central and Eastern European business development—the most rapidly growing economy in one of the fastest growing regions of the world. I was there at just the right time to witness history taking place, as Poland took the reins of its own destiny and transitioned from communism to capitalism.

The company where I worked blossomed from 50 people when I arrived to more than 1,000 by the time I moved away, just five years later. My career flourished, as I was able to launch and grow a significant number of brands in a dynamic marketing environment that I would not have experienced in a smaller, less-growth-oriented country like the Czech Republic.

I made wonderful, lifelong friends, and I was able to work and travel all over Europe. That set me up for moving to Asia as a next step, where I have now lived for 20 years.

Most importantly, on a lovely Sunday morning 17 months after arriving in Warsaw, I bumped into an American—ironically, a fellow Nebraskan whose family back home lived only a short distance from mine. A tall, striking man who, through his own series of twists and turns, found himself working in Warsaw, too. What were the odds? Two years later, when he asked me to marry him, that same little voice that had encouraged me to move to Poland quietly whispered, "Say 'yes.'" And I did. Without a doubt, he remains to this day the kind of loving, trustworthy, and loyal man who would follow me to the ends of the Earth.

I would not have experienced any of this had I not consistently listened to the Inner Coach. Looking back, I'm incredibly grateful to that brave, young version of me who, despite how bad things may have looked, chose to listen and act on a hunch. It's that same young woman who allows me to look back today on all those seemingly unrelated twists and turns, all those chaotic "jagged edges," and see the perfectly smooth, straight line that was really there.

This is an example of the type of major transition that can happen when you allow yourself to listen to the Inner Coach. But this type of guidance occurs every day for all of us, in both large and small ways.

What about you? Perhaps you felt a nudge or heard a passing comment from someone which caused you to make a change in plans that eventually turned out for the better. Maybe you attended an unexpected event only to find yourself meeting the perfect person for your new business idea.

If this seems strange to you, the truth is that for centuries, great minds from history and all walks of life have regularly reported receiving this type of intuitive guidance—people like Ben Franklin, Nikola Tesla, Albert Einstein, and Steve Jobs, not to mention myriads of famous songwriters and authors.

So what do you have to lose from trying this? Follow the nudge you feel to check out that latest art exhibit or read the book that someone randomly left on your desk. And if you do find a song repeatedly playing in your ear, by all means, pause and think about the meaning of those lyrics. You may be surprised to discover that it isn't so random after all. In fact, it may just solve a challenge you've been facing for months.

Dialing into Your Inner GPS

If you are aware of the Inner Coach and have experienced this guidance, it's likely been something you feel comes and goes. But in reality, it isn't the Inner Coach that comes and goes. It's *you*. At best, you likely tune in and out of your inner guidance with little consistency. You get a hunch only to ignore it. You accept an invitation with a sense that it's the right thing to do, but as the event approaches, you start worrying about what could go wrong, and you end up cancelling at the last minute. You wake up with an exciting inspiration that could take your career to the next level, but by noon, you've talked yourself out of exploring it.

Despite your inconsistency, your Inner Coach remains unflappable. Whether you've only occasionally accessed this guidance or you've shut it out completely by dropping into fear, you can trust your Inner Coach to be there whenever you turn to it. The Inner Coach is not the least bit swayed by your fear-based thoughts. No matter how far off-track you may go, detouring into anger, resentment, irritation, disgust—or whatever other fear-based emotion you might be experiencing—the minute you plug back into the Inner Coach, it simply recalculates and sets you back on track. It is an extraordinary resource, unlimited in its capacity for wisdom and creativity.

If you trust in the Inner Coach and listen to its guidance, you will never make the wrong choice. But, like any good coach, the Inner

Coach will never impose itself on you. You're always free to shut it out and choose fear instead.

It's important to nurture the connection with your Inner Coach. The more you cultivate it, the more you will experience it. You do this by slowing down, even if only for a moment. Allow space for it. Be open to listening. When you do feel a nudge or get an impulse, trust it, act on it, and see where it leads. Approach it with what I call "objective curiosity." That's how you begin to allow the Inner Coach to influence your life.

Learning to listen to the Inner Coach is like anything else: at first, it may seem a bit foreign. But remember that the Inner Coach is not foreign at all. It is the voice of your natural energetic state, so you're not learning anything new. You are simply re-engaging with what used to be a regular part of your life—something you knew as a child. It's in your memory, so it will come back to you. You just need to pick it back up and apply willingness, practice, and persistence.

If you think you can't hear the Inner Coach, I promise it's because you've just forgotten how. Since our default programming is most often aligned with the fear-based thought-system, we don't realize just how much we keep fear going through self-talk. Yet, if you pay attention, you'll likely notice that the voice narrating all day long is the Inner Defeatist, and you'll see how it's keeping the fear-based default programming in place. Indeed, once you start observing your thoughts, you'll probably see just how much your self-talk is a vicious-circle loop of fear and defense.

All day long you anticipate obstacles and plan how to defend against them—managing, but not leading. Unless you change your mental conversations on the inside, you're setting yourself up to stay in fear. And that feeling will drive the trajectory of your life, causing it to either stay where it is or get worse. It won't get better—if it's based on fear, it simply can't. Fear only ever results in more fear.

So, if you want to change your relationships, your career, your health, your life in general, or even the world, you must first break up with the Inner Defeatist and let go of your old, outdated beliefs. If those beliefs don't serve you in creating the life you want, it's time to kick them to the curb.

Once you break up with those thoughts, you've also got to stop talking about them to yourself. **What you focus on grows. Let your self-talk reflect what you *do* want, not what you don't.**

—10—

Changing Your Inner Dialogue

Once you start listening to your self-talk and realizing how much airtime the Inner Defeatist is getting compared to the Inner Coach, you'll likely want to make some changes to your internal conversations.

Having glimpsed what a powerful tool self-talk can be in driving outcomes in your life, let's look at the best way to use it to your advantage. To do that, you'll need to begin with a strong, foundational, JOP-based belief, what I call an "anchor belief." You can design your own, based on what feels right to you. Here's one I use regularly:

"**Everything is always working out for my greatest good.**"

Whether you choose this particular anchor belief to focus on or a different one of your own, remember that your thoughts and beliefs are energetic. As you've seen with the What-You-Think-Is-What-You-Get Pyramid, those energetic beliefs drive your outcomes.

In case you've never really focused before on the power of beliefs to drive results, I want to point out that a belief such as "everything is always working out for my greatest good" is not intended as a statement of fact. We don't have to look far to see that life is clearly not working out for a lot of people. There is an immense amount of suffering taking place.

What I *am* saying is that *it doesn't have to be that way*. The path to a future that's different from the past is achieved through remembering the forgotten choice—through choosing to make a foundational shift in thought-system. And the best way to do that is through the power of self-talk.

Through being in a JOP-based state, embracing your anchor belief, and keeping it top of mind, your self-talk programming will help you view your work and life from a completely new perspective. It will actually create the best results for you, saving you tremendous grief and angst in the process.

Let's play this out with an example.

Imagine you are in the running to gain a big, new client account. In fact, achieving your entire year's budget depends on winning this new business.

If fear is running the show, your self-talk might sound like this: "What if the client chooses a competitor? What if we miss the target? What if I have to lay off team members? What if I lose my job?"

Using the pyramid model, you can imagine how this fear-based self-talk would drive outcomes that produce the very thing you hope to avoid. Indeed, if you continue to operate within the fear-based thought-system, things are certain *not* to work out for you, in some way or other.

The obvious outcome is that you don't get the client, and all those "what ifs" become reality. Or perhaps you *do* get the client, but the experience will be one of constant stress and anxiety, with problem after problem. Remember: when we start with a fear-based belief, it can only ever result in some form of fear.

Now, let's look at what happens when you use your self-talk to fully embrace a JOP-based anchor belief such as "everything is always working out for my greatest good." This requires thoroughly shifting your energetic thought-system away from fear. Your anchor phrase cannot simply be viewed as a "positive affirmation." *It must reflect a fundamental shift in your thought-system.*

Remember the analogy shared earlier about the two energetic thought-systems being like two separate communication channels? To fully embrace such an anchor belief means that you must change the channel you've been listening to, intentionally switching your dial to the Joy of Possibility. That means changing the energy in which you are operating.

How do you do that? You hold your anchor thought front and center in your mind. More than just saying it, you think about it, continually using your self-talk to reinforce it. Anticipate it. Affirm it. Look for evidence that supports it. And most importantly, use your self-talk to create the *feeling* that everything is always, genuinely, working out for your greatest good.

If JOP is running the show, here is how your self-talk may sound: "Everything is always working out for my greatest good, and that includes this potential new client. So, I can trust my gut and stay tuned to my Inner Coach. I'm excited by and curious about the possibilities."

Can you see that using your self-talk in service of your anchor belief will help you view the situation from a completely different energetic mindset? If you *do* get the client, that's perfect. If you *don't* get the client, that's also perfect. Having embraced the JOP-based belief that everything is always working out for your greatest good, you know that whatever the result is, it's the *right* result.

Thanks to this foundational JOP-based belief, your Inner Coach is coming through loud and clear—and you can listen to it and act upon it. As a result, it turns out that everything *is* always working out for you.

The key is to trust whatever is happening. Even in the moments when it looks as if things aren't unfolding as you would like, hold tight to your foundational JOP-based belief, no matter how much everything around you seems to point in the opposite direction. When you are consistently in a state of trust, you will not only feel better about any situation, you'll also end up thinking more clearly, doing a better job, and ultimately achieving better outcomes.

That's why being in the JOP-based mindset and consistently embracing an anchor belief such as "everything is always working out for my greatest good" will drive a foundational shift in outcomes. Because all that you experience will be viewed through the lens of possibility. You will begin to look at what is happening in the present as a steppingstone for where you're going.

Is embracing this belief a guarantee that you'll always get the new client? No. But it's the ability to trust that, even if you don't get the client, there is a reason that's consistent with your anchor belief. So, instead of losing time and productivity to fear, blame, "what-ifs," and self-doubt, you are right back out there, designing your next proposal and lining up your next potential client—which might be an even better one. Think about it: if you *had* taken on that client, you wouldn't have had time to work with this new, better client that is coming into the picture.

Using self-talk to embrace a JOP-based anchor belief helps you recognize that you genuinely have nothing to fear. Repeat after me: "This is not some 'sweet sentiment' or nice 'positive thinking' approach!" Instead, this is the foundation of a profound shift in energy and thinking that can alter the trajectory of all your experiences. **You are literally retraining your belief system to work *for* you instead of *against* you.**

The Proof Is in the Results

The JOP-based belief that "everything is always working out for my greatest good" has resulted in amazing outcomes for dozens of my clients, friends, family members, and colleagues. Here is one example.

During one of the biggest economic downturns in modern history, Troy and his wife, Anna, watched in horror as the value of their home plummeted before their eyes. Troy was just beginning to recover from a lengthy illness, and between the price of medical care and skyrocketing costs of food and gas, they were feeling the pinch. Luckily for them, Troy watched their finances carefully, so they had always made good economic decisions and lived well within their means. But as the crisis dragged on, they watched their financial safety net slip away. Just when it looked like things couldn't get much worse, Troy lost his job.

They tried everything they could think of to hang on to the life they'd created. Yet with each new plan to keep their home or dig themselves out of what felt like an ever-deepening hole, solution after solution fell apart.

"Looking back, I just have to laugh at the perfection of the whole thing," Anna told me. "I had just started learning about the impact of self-talk and the choice between fear and JOP, so in the midst of all this craziness, I was trying to convince Troy how important it was to shift into believing that, despite appearances, everything really *was* working out for our greatest good."

She continued, "I'm not going to lie—at first it was a true leap in thinking, especially when we realized we would have to declare bankruptcy and let go of our home. Fortunately, we held each other up throughout. If either of us dipped into fear, the other served as a reminder that everything was working out for our greatest good. Before we knew it, we were speculating on what this 'greatest good' might look and feel like. We started to realize that if we were no longer tied to our home or to Troy's company, we could start our lives over anywhere—maybe even somewhere tropical, which is something we had always wanted to do."

The outcomes didn't arrive overnight, but ultimately, Troy and Anna's dream of living in the tropics was realized when, through a series of unfolding events, Troy found himself accepting a position with an organization located near a beautiful tropical coast. Indeed, Troy's job worked out so well that he more than doubled his salary within three years.

Today, Anna tells me, "Life is good! We love where we live, and we enjoy our wonderful lifestyle. Best of all, now that we've learned to fully embrace the belief that everything is always working out for our greatest good, we're so much more relaxed. What first appeared to be a disaster turned out to be an undeniable gift. These days, we're pretty fearless. We approach change and what the future might bring with a sense of joyful curiosity."

Pause and consider this story, as well as the story of my move to Poland. Neither of these results would have occurred if there hadn't been a foundational shift in thinking. It was the shift from fear into the energetic state of JOP that drove the outcomes. Embracing an anchor belief based on the Joy of Possibility *is* the shift in energy that sets things in motion—just as embracing fear-based beliefs will lead to fear-based outcomes.

Perhaps you've witnessed this happen to someone you know, or perhaps it has even happened to you: a relationship ended abruptly, you lost your job, your finances took a hit, or you had to give up your home. If you process what happened through fear-based beliefs such as "it's not fair; these things always seem to happen to me; life is out to get me," you're likely to feel anger and victimization, followed by behaviors of blame, attack, or defense. The outcome of that fear-based belief process? No better job comes along, the relationship you desire eludes you, the move to your dream location never materializes, and on and on.

Once the impact of a JOP-based anchor belief has been realized, dozens of clients have noted how this new JOP-based self-talk not only changes the outcomes they experience, but they are actually able to see the beauty of it as it's happening *in real time*. They no longer have to wait years to understand it in hindsight. When seen in this new light, the past begins to look and feel different as well. Events or situations that made no sense at the time seem perfectly clear once viewed through the energetic lens of the Joy of Possibility.

Here's a case in point: Ram came into my office, frustrated with his boss, Lee. Having worked for Lee for almost eight years, Ram shared, "Lee never helps me and never teaches me what I need to know to succeed in this company. I always have to fend for myself and figure out everything on my own. I end up making mistakes and doing twice the amount of work that Lee does. I'm fed up with it!"

When I asked Ram if he had discussed this with his boss, he responded with, "There's no point! I tried in the past, but it's clear to me that Lee isn't going to change. I've gone over this in my mind hundreds of times, but I just don't see any other possible outcomes: either I leave, or I'm stuck working for a bad boss."

I then shared with Ram the important role that self-talk plays in reinforcing existing thoughts and beliefs and the impact that has on our results.

"Let's look at this through the lens of possibility," I suggested. "What are all the reasons why Lee's lack of help over the past eight years has been *positive* for you? Write down the longest list possible."

It took Ram about 30 seconds to shift out of fear and into the energy of possibility, but once he did, the reasons started flowing: when Ram didn't get support from Lee, Ram often reached out to others, which had resulted in him building an excellent internal and external network. Because Ram often needed to figure out issues on his own, he had become more efficient with his workload, handling more tasks in less time. Given the way it felt to be on the receiving end of Lee's leadership style, Ram made an extra effort to ensure that his team members felt supported when they needed him, giving him a good reputation as a strong leader.

By the time Ram was done creating the list, he had uncovered 15 specific ways that Lee's seemingly "frustrating" behaviors had helped Ram succeed even more than he would have otherwise. In fact, at the end of our conversation, Ram described the experience of the past eight years as "absolutely perfect."

To help Ram stay aligned with this new Joy-of-Possibility outlook, I asked, "Based on what you've just uncovered, what self-talk could you use moving forward to reinforce this insight?"

After a bit of back-and-forth, Ram answered, "I trust my career is unfolding exactly as it should, and everything that happens is an opportunity to grow and learn."

When Ram came to see me, he was operating under the belief that he was a victim of his boss—a belief that was being reinforced regularly through his internal self-talk. This caused his fear-based thoughts to seem more and more real every day. But that belief was false, and once he realized this, Ram was able to use self-talk to his benefit, helping him shift perspectives and drive new outcomes.

So, take control of your self-talk by changing the nature of your inner conversations. Through regularly choosing to listen to the Inner Coach and following its guidance, you will recognize events unfolding in "a perfectly straight line." And once you do, life becomes a full-on adventure.

—11—

Why It Seems
So Hard to Shift

As you probably recognize by now, making the transition from fear to the Joy of Possibility is a game-changer. Given how negative and stressed most of us report feeling, you would think we'd all be clamoring at the chance to get out of fear and into the possibility of *what could be*. Yet as much as we hate the results of our fear-based thought-system, giving it up can evoke … well, fear.

The most obvious reason we find it hard to let go of fear is that *we believe in it*. But there are also other reasons that make this shift seem difficult.

Reason #1: We have a strong desire to be right

As we've seen, our thoughts and beliefs serve as "mental scaffolding" of sorts. They support who we think we are as well as how we believe life works. Because of this, we tend to cling to existing thoughts and beliefs, even when they hold us back from experiencing the outcomes we want.

This is why shifting away from fear can seem so difficult. Whenever we experience fear, our impulse is to hold on desperately to our existing scaffolding, insisting on how everything needs to be by clinging to the the way it has always been and believing firmly that we are right. The problem is that relying on our mental scaffolding—which is built on the foundations of fear-based thoughts and beliefs—results in binding us even more firmly to fear.

Nonetheless, we mistakenly believe that if we can just dig our heels in deep enough and prove that our fear-based beliefs are *right*, this will somehow propel us out of the fear.

Our need to be right is so strong that even when we feel miserable about what we believe to be true, we still experience a strange sense of security from proving ourselves right.

For example:

- You believe that your marriage has lost its spark, so you stop trying, keeping you and your spouse's relationship the same, and confirming your belief.

- You're certain that your assistant will forget something crucial before your big meeting, so you message him non-stop, causing him to doubt himself and forget something.

- You believe your kids don't appreciate you, so every time you do something for them, you remind them: "I did this for you, you know—not that you'd ever appreciate me for it," which results in them feeling more guilt and resentment than appreciation.

- You know that if you want something done right, you'd better do it yourself. So you don't ask for help and then feel unsupported when you have to do everything on your own.

- You believe that a particular deal is too good to be true, and you're just sure something will go wrong with it. So you don't put in your best effort and then feel justified when it all falls apart.

How else do we reinforce our existing thinking? We only watch YouTube videos or television channels that we know align with our current beliefs. We only listen to podcasts that say what we want to hear. When we are presented with a thought that doesn't support our beliefs, we don't listen to it—we simply ignore it. We stop seeking new information, innovative ideas, or contrasting ways of thinking because we strongly believe that we already "know."

Here's an example of this phenomenon that I see frequently: There is a point in my coaching process when I present clients with a summary of verbal feedback from their input providers. There is almost always a longer list of strengths than weaknesses, but clients typically seem impatient when listening to their virtues. In contrast, when I share with clients their development areas, they pay much closer attention.

What's that about? It demonstrates our desire to improve, certainly. But I think it also relates to our need to be right. So-called "bad" feedback supports what we tend to believe about ourselves—matching the self-talk we hear when we listen to the Inner Defeatist. In other words, we pay more attention to evidence that supports our fear-based belief that we're not good enough rather than focusing on evidence that suggests we're doing well.

Reason #2: We're attached to a particular outcome

Because of our strong need to be right, we can easily become attached to a specific outcome—a clear indicator that fear is lurking underneath. After all, the more afraid we are, the more we try to control what happens, leading us to become attached to a particular result. In turn, that often produces an attitude of "my way or the highway," stunting creativity and killing chances for opportunity and growth.

Similarly, because fear would have us see limitations instead of possibilities, when we listen to the Inner Defeatist, we tend to label everything as either "right" (which feels safe) or "wrong" (which feels dangerous). So, we also cling to specific outcomes in hopes of assuring safety.

Reason #3: We think we're being victimized

Another key reason it can seem so hard to shift out of fear and into JOP is the ingrained belief that our experience of the world comes from outside of us. We've been taught to believe that the outcomes of our lives are almost completely at the mercy of others—especially anyone we see as an authority figure.

Because of this, when given the choice of listening to the Inner Coach or listening to an external "authority," we most often choose to override our internal guidance and defer instead to the perceived external authority.

As a result, we see ourselves as powerless in the face of the world "out there." We say things like, "That's just the way it is," "It's not up to me," or "Those are simply the rules." We've been trained to think that what we see and experience outside of ourselves is evidence of how things are, which leads us to believe that what happens to us is in the hands of external decision-makers. But it isn't. It's simply evidence of where we've been focusing our thoughts and beliefs. And as long as we continue to believe that the cause of everything is outside of ourselves, we will see ourselves as victims.

Reason #4: We focus on what we *don't* want

Even if we do take time to get clear on what we want, we typically focus the bulk of our attention on what we will have to overcome in order to get it. Instead of placing our creative energy on building what we truly desire, we point the spotlight on all the roadblocks and challenges we will have to conquer and the many hurdles we'll have to jump over in order to get to where we want to go.

We focus on finding what's wrong. Even some motivational speakers use phrases like, "What's the worst than can happen?" This is because we've been mistakenly taught to believe that, somehow, by giving all our attention to what we *don't* want, we will be able to create what we *do* want.

We end up spending our days trying to achieve our dreams by managing our fears. We become inspired by a new business idea and then give all our attention to what might stand in the way of turning it into reality. We want to get into better shape, but instead of focusing on how good we'll feel as we eat well and incorporate exercise back into our lives, we give all our attention to the food and drinks we'll have to give up and how hard it will be to fit exercise into our schedule. As long as we continue to operate this way, we give our energy to fear, blocking us from shifting into the Joy of Possibility.

Remember: what you focus on grows. So directing where you place your energy and attention is critical—it's an "inside job" requiring the most important form of leadership.

—12—

The Most Important Form of Leadership

We drive one-and-a-half-ton automobiles on highways at speeds of up to 130 kph/80 mph. Conductors whisk dozens of railcars through towns at speeds of up to 260 kph/160 mph. Pilots propel 600-ton planes through the air at 800 kph/500 mph. Once again, our ancestors would be in absolute awe of such impressive feats.

But these machines pale in comparison to the most powerful force we can control. That distinction belongs to the mind.

The Forgotten Choice is about learning how to harness that magnificent mind of yours to your benefit, empowering you to embrace a system of thought that works *for* you instead of *against* you. **This calls for leadership.**

We often think of leadership as influencing or controlling something outside of ourselves: people, a business, a team, a family, a group, a community, or government. But the most important leadership is not external—it's *internal*. I'm referring to *self*-leadership, the foundation of all leadership. After all, you cannot be a good leader of anyone or anything else unless you first lead yourself successfully.

I believe **the new frontier in leadership will occur at the micro level—through individual leadership of the mind.** There is no other form of leadership that is more important, because it's key to all that happens in our lives. I call this *Mind Leadership*®.

In today's world, Mind Leadership is more critical than ever. Thanks to modern technology, we are living in an age of distraction, regularly shifting rapidly from reading an email on a laptop, to texting on a cell phone, to glancing at a ticker-tape running across the bottom of a television screen, to checking social media accounts, to watching a YouTube video—all while listening to music through ear buds. This process of quickly shifting our focus means that the average attention span—our ability to spend time continuously focused on a single task—is dropping. In fact, some estimate it has fallen to as little as eight seconds (reportedly one second less than the attention span of a goldfish).

This nonstop access to media also means that we are more aware than ever of what is going on in our world. We immediately find out about deaths in far-flung countries or earthquakes two continents away, not to mention political unrest, police brutality, animal cruelty, wildfires, mud slides, and cars floating down flooded streets. And if that isn't enough, just open up your web browser and search any topic. You'll find hundreds of thousands—if not millions—of entries.

In short, more than any other time in history, we are experiencing an information overload that has resulted in an epidemic-like inability to focus. It's hardly surprising that more and more people say they feel overwhelmed.

This continuous and unprecedented consumption of tragedy, distraction, and threat can easily cause us to believe there is more to be afraid of every day. We certainly have more ready access to events that can *induce* fear. If we let it, that constant access can distract us from the most important thing we can keep in mind at any point in time: the forgotten choice. So how we approach this modern-day challenge requires good, solid Mind Leadership.

Mind Leadership versus Mind Management

Most people talk about mind *management,* but besides the nice alliteration, think about it: what does a *manager* do versus a *leader*? In his book *On Becoming a Leader*, Warren Bennis includes a list of the differences between the two titles. Briefly:

- A manager administers, coordinates, and organizes

- A leader grows, develops, and inspires

When a mind is being *managed*—organized, administered, and coordinated—there's a tendency to want to keep doing the same things over and over again, like a good soldier. But in today's world of constant external disruption, what we need instead is Mind *Leadership*—truly taking charge and inspiring the mind toward growth and future possibility.

Which would you rather have—a mind that is administered, organized, and coordinated? Or a mind that is led, inspired, and focused on development?

Taking time to focus on developing your Mind Leadership—the ultimate form of self-leadership—is foundational to all future success. And a key means of strengthening your Mind Leadership is finding time for mental breaks.

Mind Rest

Whenever I'm not traveling, I exercise with trainers four days a week. I like to try different kinds of workouts, so over the years, I've worked with at least two dozen different fitness experts. At the end of sessions, every instructor says the same thing: "Make sure you get some rest between now and your next workout."

We all know our bodies need rest. Research shows that if you go too long without sleep, you lose your ability to focus, you stop making sense, you gain weight, and you fall ill. So why don't we also give our *minds* rest?

Many people say that genuine mind rest seems almost impossible. We have trained our minds to be running every day, all day. And if by chance our schedules do open up for possible mind-break time, we pick up a gadget to make sure we are always mentally occupied. We "avoid the void" like the plague, finding any excuse available to keep our minds busy. In fact, many clients report that their smartphone is the last thing they look at before falling asleep and the first thing they reach for when they wake up.

But just like our physical selves, our mental selves also need to take a break. Pause and reflect … how often do you give your mind genuine rest?

You may be asking yourself what genuine "mind rest" really means. As mentioned before, our minds are typically operating in rapid-refocus mode, creating a frenetic energy that comes from quickly shifting our concentration from one thing to another. So true mind rest involves giving your mind genuine, single-minded focus time.

Through the process of writing this book, I have personally come to appreciate the importance of mental breaks. At the beginning of the writing phase, a flood of ideas came through, but unfortunately, they always seemed to arrive in the middle of the night, disrupting my sleep. As an author, when any idea is powerful enough to wake me up, I know better than to say to myself, "I'll just stay here in my bed, cozy and warm, and I'll write down that idea in the morning." Experience tells me I'll never remember it. So in order to capture those great, late-night ideas, I have to wake up, turn on a light, grab a pad of paper, pick up a pen, and write them down. By the time I'm done, I'm wide awake, and I lose even more sleep.

For months on end, a flow of middle-of-the-night ideas kept coming through, seriously taking a hit on my sleep time. Finally, one day, I paused and asked a simple question, "Why aren't these ideas coming through during the day when I'm already awake?" That's when the patient, still, and always-calm voice of the Inner Coach quietly replied, "Rest your mind enough during the day to allow ideas to come through, and you'll be able to sleep through the night." Fair point. From then on, I started taking daytime mind-rest periods more consistently, and the book ideas began to flow during waking hours.

So how do you practice mind rest? By providing your mind with short periods of extreme focus, starting with one minute and expanding from there.

> **Give yourself one-minute mind-rest breaks every hour.**

Set your clock or phone to ping you on the hour; then spend one minute—just 60 seconds—sitting quietly. During that one minute, bring your shoulders down. Relax your body. Take two or three deep breaths. Then find one thing to focus on. It could be the feeling of your breath going in and out of your nostrils. Maybe you stare at a still object outside the window. Perhaps you focus on the sound of cars driving by outside or the whirr of a nearby fan. Or you could hold a pen in your hand and study it intently. Whatever. The key is to give your mind time to fully focus on one single thing.

During this time, if you notice your thoughts going back to some drama from the past or fast-forwarding to a potential event in the future, just recognize it, be patient with yourself, and return to your focal point. Remember that it's only 60 seconds—those thoughts will still be waiting for you when you're done with your one-minute break.

Regular mind rest periods help you succeed in taking charge of your mind and leading it. And one minute per hour of mind rest during your waking hours will give you about 16 minutes of mind rest per day. That's 16 more minutes than most people get.

Just like a muscle in your body, if you give your mind rest after exercising it, it will come back stronger, supporting you in developing Mind Leadership.

Do We Truly Not Have Time for Mind Rest?

No matter how simple finding 60 spare seconds per hour may seem, many people say, "I don't have time for mind-rest breaks. I wake up, hit the ground running with work and family, and I go, go, go until I collapse into bed at night. That's just the kind of life I lead."

Our world does seem busier than ever. And yet, reflecting back on the lives of our ancestors, it's fascinating to compare. Just a few generations back (indeed, for most of human existence), we would have spent morning until night on survival activities— growing our food in order to eat, building a fire in order to cook, making fabric to create our clothes, milling our own wheat to make bread, pumping a well to get water, and on and on.

Think about it: in just the last 100 years, the number of modern comforts has increased rapidly, dramatically improving the quality of our day-to-day lives. Keeping in mind these extraordinary conveniences, our lives *should* be filled with an abundance of non-survival "free time."

But again, whenever a spare moment does appear, we grab our phones, surf the internet, play games, or binge-watch our favorite TV shows. It seems we will do anything to distract ourselves from taking mental breaks.

So, we *can* find the time to practice mind rest. The key is to be motivated enough to do it. That motivation will hopefully come from realizing that a one-minute mental break per hour is so much more valuable than using that minute to check an inbox.

Once you experience the positive impact of genuine mind-rest periods, you may wonder why you haven't taken them sooner.

The more you train your mind with regular rest, the more you set yourself up for successful Mind Leadership and learning how to stay in the moment. After all, you can only experience JOP and create the life you really want if you're fully in the *present*.

—13—

The Undeniable Satisfaction of Being in the Present

In our mind, we can only be in one of three time periods at any moment:

- The past (which is over)

- The future (which hasn't happened yet)

- The present (which is occurring right now)

Humans spend inordinate amounts of time in the past and in the future. There is probably no other species on the planet that does this. Can you imagine a Labrador Retriever fretting over what to serve the Dachshunds when they come over for dinner next Saturday? No, animals just live in the moment. But we humans spend surprisingly little time there, truly being aware and experiencing what is happening *in the present*.

The Past

Do you remember Pauline, who shared during a coaching session that she was lying awake at night, reliving again and again something she had said at work that had blown up in her face? She was losing sleep over it, and it was taking a hit on her confidence.

Perhaps you've done this, too. We agonize over something that took place in the past, reliving an argument we had, regretting something we did, staying angry about something someone said to us or an event that took place years ago. Wouldn't it be nice if, like computers, we could occasionally press the "undo" button? But of course, we can't. The past is simply that—in the *past*—and it can't be changed.

Even though we know we can't change the past, we regularly go back in time and relive former experiences. And since we cannot change history, reliving an experience simply causes us to wallow in the drama and the problems of that event, none of which will ever change. It's a tremendous waste of time and energy.

"But, wait a minute!" some might say. "The past teaches us, so reviewing it is a *good* thing, right?"

It can be, absolutely. But how the past teaches us—and maybe even more importantly, what ends up being learned—depends entirely on the energetic thought-system we embrace during the review process.

When we look back on past events through the lens of the fear-based thought-system, two things typically happen:

- First, we approach the experience from the belief that *something went wrong*.

- Second, since we believe something went wrong, we go over the past in our mind, reviewing *behaviors or external factors* in order to figure out what to *do* differently in the future:

  ○ What did I (or someone else) do that caused this to happen?

  ○ What could I have done or said to prevent this from happening?

  ○ What would I do or say differently if I could relive it all over again?

Whenever we reflect back on something by focusing mainly on behaviors or external factors, the takeaways tend to sound like this: "I learned that ...

- ... I'll never do that again."

- ... I'll never say that again."

- ... I should never have trusted him."

- ... I need to keep my mouth shut."

- ... I need to watch my back more carefully next time."

- ... I shouldn't show vulnerability."

And on and on.

Until we are aware of how the two foundational energetic thought-systems drive outcomes, it's only logical that we would place our focus and attention on the *observable*—trying to pinpoint the specific behavior that caused the "bad" results.

But as these examples demonstrate, whenever we link cause to behavior alone, it limits us. We tend to become overly cautious, hold back, or even shut down, afraid of saying or doing the wrong thing. That results in a fear-based preoccupation with "messing up," blocking us from accessing the Inner Coach and holding us back from our natural ability to operate in the Joy of Possibility.

We experience what we focus on. So, while we can't change the past, we *can* change the way we reflect on it by looking at it through a JOP-based lens. Once you embrace a what-could-be approach, you get out of the limiting, fear-based mindset of what-went-wrong and instead move into the Joy of Possibility, which stimulates growth and expansion. Looking at the past through the Joy of Possibility sounds like this:

- What potential do I see now after having had that experience?

- Keeping in mind that everything is always working out for my greatest good, how do I view this situation from my current perspective?

- In what ways was that past event perfect for me?

- How did what happened help me grow and/or set me up for success?

- What beliefs did I have going into that experience that I could change in the future?

It's all in how we look at it. Shift away from the belief that behaviors or external factors are the causes of outcomes, and instead examine what belief or thought created that past result. That's how those previous experiences can become amazing, forward-focused teachers.

The Future

We are incredibly good at making up stories about what might happen in the future, playing out "what if" tales in our mind. That's living life like a chess game, always strategizing, trying to decide the next move. "If I do this, then he might do that. If he does, then what move should I make next to stay a step ahead?" This type of thinking can drive us mad, yet we do it, day-in and day-out.

Over time, we begin to think we're good at the game. We come to see our ability to stay a step or two ahead of our fears as some kind of positive skillset. The problem is that instead of lessening our fear, this approach actually *reinforces* it, and we become increasingly terrified to let our guard down. Why? Because even though we may be good at the game, we're still playing the game of fear.

The Present

Whether you spend more time in the past (rehashing what happened minutes, hours, months, or years ago) or spend more time looking ahead (conjecturing and dramatizing about the future), both are woefully unsatisfying and can't compare to being truly in the present, where you can enjoy and benefit from the Joy of Possibility in the moment.

That's because JOP only exists in the here-and-now. And since the Inner Coach is the voice for JOP, **you can only hear your Inner Coach when you are fully present.**

Where Are You Now?

This lack of being present regularly plays out in our lives. You attend a meeting but constantly glance at your phone. You finally get some quality one-on-one time with your daughter, only to find yourself mentally preoccupied with a work issue. As a third example, perhaps you recognize yourself in this cartoon?

Another illustration: you're halfway to the office and suddenly can't remember if you turned off the iron, shut off the stove, turned on the alarm system, or closed the garage door.

Or have you ever misplaced something—your keys, a pair of socks, your cell phone, or an important document? When this happens, the Inner Defeatist would have you believe that your mind is slipping. You start to wonder if perhaps it's because of stress or maybe your age is starting to show. But all this *really* tells you is that you weren't paying attention to where you placed those items at the time you placed them. You were not fully *present*.

Several years ago, I went through a phase of misplacing things, to the tune of three or four items per week. It was so annoying! Recognizing this was happening because I wasn't being fully present, I began a new Mind Leadership habit: as I placed anything anywhere, I paused for one second, brought my awareness to the present, and said either to myself or out loud, "I'm placing my keys on the table." "My cell phone is now sitting on my desk." "This contract to review is now located underneath my computer monitor." Guess what? My "forgetfulness" evaporated.

I encourage clients to do this, too. They have come up with phrases such as, "I'm focusing on what's happening at this meeting," "I'm centered on being with family right now," and "I am here and enjoying my holiday today."

Remember: being present and fully aware is a choice that only takes a second. Give it a try, and you'll likely find improvements in both your productivity and your peace of mind.

The Impact of Reliving the Past in the Present

You know from the What-You-Think-Is-What-You-Get Pyramid that what you focus on, think about, and believe in the present is what creates your future. So, every time you recall something from the past, you are bringing that experience back into the present by reactivating the same energy you experienced at the time it originally happened. Likewise, you experience the same feelings and, as a result, you will get the same outcomes all over again.

This is how you keep the past alive in your current reality. You actually *reinforce* your past as a basis for recreating it in the future. The past then becomes the present, and the present becomes the future, keeping you in a repetitive cycle.

If you find yourself saying, "Why is this always happening to me?" or if you continuously wonder why the same destructive patterns keep recurring in your life no matter how hard you try to avoid them, this is likely the answer. This past-present-future pattern is also in large part why history repeats itself.

You can switch out of this cycle. Because the Joy of Possibility is the thought-system of potentiality, shifting into JOP allows you to create what you want. In fact, the *only* surefire way to get what you desire is to get into the Joy of Possibility. That can only be done in the present, because it is what you experience from moment to moment (through thinking, believing, and feeling) that creates your future.

—14—

Creating Your Future Is Easier Than You Think

As young children, we often believe that the sky is the limit. That's because we are more frequently in a state of JOP at that age, where everything does seem possible.

Then, as life goes on and we get a bit of experience under our belts, fear takes over as our learned default system. That state of "possibility" seems to wane, and we forget we have a natural ability to create our future.

It's easy to interpret this shift in mindset as simply growing up and becoming "more realistic," but actually, something bigger is at play: once we start allowing fear to be our guiding mindset, we constantly live in an "on-guard" state and find ourselves *managing* our lives, completely losing touch with our innate ability to *lead* our lives.

Having learned that the combination of energy, thoughts, and feelings are at the base of all that you experience, you can now see the power of bringing together these elements and creating what you want. Instead of waiting for life to happen "to" you (where you act and react like a victim), you can intentionally get in the driver's seat, take charge, and bring what you want into existence.

To shift from where you are to where you want to be, you must be crystal clear on what it is you want: your vision for the future in all areas of your life. The key to doing so is yet another aspect of Mind Leadership—to imagine your future vividly, with focused attention. This is called *visioning*, or *creative visualization*. Used regularly by many professionals, such as athletes and actors, this practice works because what we think and feel in the present creates what we experience in the future.

If by chance you think visioning is the stuff of fairy dust and magic wands, consider this: **visioning is nothing new. You've been visioning since you were born—in fact, your thoughts and beliefs have created the existence you have now.**

But most of us have not been visioning *consciously,* so the key to success lies in bringing this to our awareness, and then deliberately focusing our energy. When we do, we can shift to *leading* ourselves from within the energetic state of the Joy of Possibility, because that is where the potentiality of "what could be" exists. Using the JOP-based thought-system, you become a conscious, deliberate creator of your future.

Just how powerful is visioning? One of my favorite examples is a story about Walt Disney. He died in 1966, only 11 years after the opening of Disneyland. Years later, after the theme park was fully built up and Walt Disney World had been opened, the story goes that someone approached Mike Vance, Creative Director for Walt Disney Studios at the time, and said, "Isn't it too bad that Walt didn't live to see this?" Without skipping a beat, Mike replied, "But he *did* see it, and that's why it's here."

Never underestimate the power of your mind's ability to create. As Albert Einstein said, "Imagination is the greatest creative force in the universe."

The Usual Reasons Why Visioning Exercises Fail to Deliver

Perhaps you've heard of visioning exercises, and maybe you've even tried to create a vision or two. Maybe it didn't work for you, so you decided it's useless. I hear that often: "I tried visioning, but it was a waste of time."

Here are the main reasons I believe most visioning exercises fail:

- Millions of people around the world haven't allowed themselves to consider their true potential.

- Most of us are rarely crystal-clear about what we really want. We spend more time focusing on what we *don't* want.

- We don't know how to vision, and/or we've not been given the best guidelines for visioning success.

- We think we can simply visualize (without feelings) and get what we want. But visualizing on its own does nothing except create daydreams.

- We spend most of our time recreating the same outcomes over and over again because we're thinking the same thoughts from one day to the next.

- Since we revisit the past by constantly remembering it and bringing it back into the present, that creates the same patterns in the future. As a result, we don't create anything *new*.

- Whenever we *do* think about the future, we invent fear-based stories, looking ahead and fretting about what might happen.

However, under the right direction and with the right guidelines, conscious, JOP-based visioning can bring extraordinary results.

Your "Ideal Day" Vision

To help you gain clarity on what you want the future to look like, here is an exercise that has produced amazing outcomes for both me and my clients: create a vision of your ideal day. You will imagine, in great detail, a day in the future when you have achieved exactly what you want. Picture that day, from morning until night. What would that experience be like? This is your ideal day, so make sure to dream big.

Further ahead, you will find a list of questions to ask yourself as you create your ideal day. Before you try this, let's review the process of how the exercise works and what you can expect as an outcome.

Your vision—your answers in response to the upcoming questions —can be written, visual, or a combination of both. Decide your preferred approach, asking yourself which form will most inspire you consistently. If you decide to use visuals, it's important that each picture or drawing should not only represent something specific to you but should also inspire a *feeling* within you.

As you get ready to create your ideal-day vision, be sure to carve out concentrated, quiet time for the vision-creation process. To prevent any interruptions, set your cell phone to silent and turn off email inbox notifications.

When you start the exercise, read the question, then take a moment to form a response to that question in your mind. You can ask each question one at a time or pose to yourself a series of questions. Some people find it helpful to close their eyes when imagining, allowing their ideal day to unfold in their mind. Whatever approach you decide upon, once you are clear, write your answers in prose or story format, or find a visual that resonates with you and represents the experience.

Go ahead and read through the questions now, but hold off starting to create your vision until you've had a chance to read the eight Vision-Creation Guidelines (which you'll find following this list of questions).

As you wake up, look around you—where are you located? What does it feel like to wake up knowing that you are fully living the life you want? What's the first thing you see as you open your eyes? What are the sounds you hear? As you get out of bed, what is going through your mind? What is your mood—your predominant feeling? How does your morning unfold? Who do you interact with first? What kinds of conversations do you have, and how do you feel during these conversations? Do you start with some form of Mind Leadership practice or physical exercise? If so, what is the experience of that? What do you have for breakfast, and how does it taste to you? When you pick out clothes to wear, how do those clothes feel in your hands? What are you wearing, and what does that feel like?

Continuing through the morning, how does it play out before you? Is it planned, or is it spontaneous? What kind of work do you do, if any? Do you drive to your work, or are you already in the location where you work (such as a home office)? What kind of environment exists in your workspace? What's the general feeling of the place, the sights, the sounds? Are you working by yourself, or as part of a team? If there's a team, what are your team members like, and how do you interact with them? What are the emotions that elicits in you? As you approach lunchtime, who will you eat with, if anybody, and how does what you eat taste? Most importantly, how does it feel to be enjoying that lunch?

How does the afternoon unfold? What is the overriding feeling as you continue throughout the day? Are you working, enjoying free time, or doing something else? What activities are you drawn to as part of your ideal day? Continuing on with your late afternoon, what happens as you get ready to finish up your workday, if that applies? Who do you see, and where do you go?

Who do you have dinner with and where? Is music playing in the background? If so, what are you hearing? What's the ambiance of the place where you're eating? What's the predominant feeling during your meal? What do you smell as the food is being prepared? What kinds of interactions do you have during and after your dinner? Are you involved in any hobbies or evening events that are special? What are the emotions that come with those activities and events?

As you get ready to finish your ideal day, what late-night, pre-bed, JOP-based habits or rituals do you have? Do you end the day reading a book, listening to music, practicing mind rest, or something else? As you crawl into bed, what do the sheets feel like? Reflecting back on how your day unfolded, what are you most grateful for? How do you know it's been the perfect day for you? What made it so special? As you start to close your eyes, what is your final inner dialogue of the day? What is the last thought that goes through your mind, and how does that feel?

This process of creating a vision and turning it into reality absolutely works. How do I know? I'm not only regularly living my own ideal-day vision, but I've also coached hundreds of senior-level executives in this technique. Though a few clients may be skeptical at first, they are continuously happy with how visioning works to create the desired outcomes they want. Year after year, I receive emails and text messages saying, "I just reread my vision day, and I'm absolutely living it, word for word!"

People are usually surprised when their visions become reality. I'm not. If you do this in the way outlined below, you can't fail to create what you desire, because the thoughts, beliefs, and feelings you experience in the present are what shape your future. This is simply the way we operate.

Vision-Creation Guidelines

Below are the eight most important principles for success in crafting an ideal-day vision. Embrace these, and you'll be soundly on your way to turning the future you want into reality.

Vision-Creation Guideline #1: Get clear about the *intent* of your vision. As you begin creating your vision, it's important to ask yourself *why* you want what you want. Though this may seem obvious, we often don't realize that what looks like a vision for your dream future might actually be based on fear.

For example, let's say your vision includes moving very far away. What is the intent? Is it because you love that area of the world and have always felt drawn to it, or is it to avoid ever having to run into your ex? Or maybe your vision includes building your own wildly successful business. What is it for? Is it because you have an idea or product you believe will make the world a better place, or is it because you want to win the approval of relatives or school mates who never thought you'd amount to much?

At each step of the way as you write your vision, double-check that your intent is genuinely founded in the Joy of Possibility.

Vision-Creation Guideline #2: **Create your vision in** *present* **tense, not future tense.** As we've learned, JOP—the energy in which our creative potential lies—only exists in the present. So, when crafting your vision, it's important to write present-tense phrases (such as, "I *am* …," "My job *is* …," "I *enjoy* …") If you use words such as "I *will*," "I *want*," "My life *will be*," "I *hope to*," or "I *anticipate*," you will simply create more want, hope, and anticipation, rather than the experience of what you really want. Remember: what you think (in the present) is what you get. So write and imagine your ideal day as if it's happening right now.

Vision-Creation Guideline #3: **Focus on the feelings you are experiencing and how you are** *being,* **not just on what you are** *doing.* We know through the What-You-Think-Is-What-You-Get Pyramid that what you feel is critical to delivering the outcomes you want. In creating a vision, the secret sauce is focusing on the emotions you experience throughout your ideal day—how you feel as you go through your vision in your mind. So, don't just capture what you will *do*. Let yourself feel how you would *be* during this ideal day. After all, we are human "beings," not human "doings."

In your mind, as you walk through your ideal-vision day, ask yourself: "What emotions do I experience when I wake up and as I have breakfast? When I interact with friends or family? When I walk into my office and observe my dedicated and capable team doing their jobs with excellence? What does it feel to be living my ideal life?" It's vital to include feelings at every step—and not just to write them down, but to *imagine* the events of the day in such detail and so vividly that you actually *experience* those emotions now.

Vision-Creation Guideline #4: Focus on how *you* are feeling, not on the emotions of others. We don't have dominion over how others feel; the only emotions we can control are our own. So, when creating your vision, pinpoint *your* emotions with phrases such as "I am excited …" "I am confident …" "I am relaxed …" Avoid focusing on others' feelings with phrases like "My family is content," "My team is passionate," "The board seems happy with my contributions," or "My neighbor seems happy."

However, your vision can (and should) reflect how others *demonstrate* to you how they feel. Do your children laugh more? Is there more collaboration among your team members? Did you receive a congratulatory note from a board member? Did your neighbor jovially invite you over for a drink? Once you've added those experiences to your ideal day, then be sure to integrate how they make *you* feel.

Vision-Creation Guideline #5: Populate your vision day with the presence of positives rather than the absence of negatives. In general, we are more experienced at figuring out what we *don't* want than what we *do* want. Sentences like "I leave work early without feeling guilty," or "I don't have to deal with conflict at home" are examples of vision statements that are fear-based and emphasize the absence of a negative (in these examples, avoiding the negativity of guilt or conflict).

Instead, in your visioning sentences, focus on what you *do* want, integrating the Joy of Possibility through the presence of positives: "I leave work early with a sense of peace, knowing that my team has everything under control." "I walk into the house feeling comfortable, knowing it's going to be a relaxing and peaceful evening."

When writing your vision, here are a few more examples of how to turn the absence of a (fear-based) negative into the presence of a (JOP-based) positive:

- *Absence of a negative:* "My partner and I don't argue about the children."
- *Presence of a positive:* "My partner and I chat openly and easily about how to raise our children."

- *Absence of a negative:* "I don't have to micromanage my team."
- *Presence of a positive:* "My team members handle their tasks expertly and independently."

- *Absence of a negative:* "I don't have to rush to get where I'm going."
- *Presence of a positive:* "I arrive in plenty of time, feeling calm and confident."

Vision-Creation Guideline #6: **Create a holistic vision of your life; don't focus on just one or two areas.** All the various parts of our lives are intricately linked, so your desired vision should be, too. What do you want for yourself personally, professionally, emotionally, mentally, and physically? Lay out what you desire in your friends, life mate/spouse, family, work, career, hobbies, charity and community involvement, and so on.

When clients craft their visions, they occasionally leave out important personal aspects. One common mistake is beginning and ending their vision day by talking about their work. But what about the period from the time you wake until you leave for the office? What about connecting with friends and/or family at the end of the day? Be sure to include a "surround-sound," 360-degree view of your life when creating the vision of your ideal day.

Vision-Creation Guideline #7: **Make your ideal day truly "ideal."** Living your ideal reality may seem so far off to you that it's hard to imagine what such a future would be like. In some visions, I've seen phrases like "I start my day by checking my phone for emails," or "Only a few mistakes are made by my direct reports." Is that what you *really* believe is "ideal?" Wouldn't you rather envision a day where you start off with a nice walk or a jog in the park? Wouldn't you rather fully embrace that you'll be relaxed because your team always delivers excellence? Check yourself if you start to make your vision anything less than perfect. This is your chance to create a future that you truly desire.

Vision-Creation Guideline #8: **Be sure to stretch your vision— reach for the stars.** A vision is created from an energy of possibility, so this is your chance to unleash your imagination and shape the existence you really want. You can create anything you desire—nothing is off limits.

Stretch yourself and aim for significant improvement, not just baby steps. Make note of everything that has changed in this ideal life of yours, including what you are thinking, how you are being, and what you are doing that's strikingly different from today. Include how you relate to others, how others relate to you, and how different you feel on this ideal day, both personally and professionally.

If your vision only brings incremental improvement to your life as it already is today, take it as a sign and stretch your imagination further.

Using Your Vision

Think of your freshly crafted vision day as your new North Star—the destination where you are headed. Now that you're clear on *what* you want to achieve, it's time to focus on *how* to get there. Here are some simple tips to help you turn your vision into reality:

- Place constant reminders of your vision everywhere you look. Keep a copy in your pocket or purse so that you will remember what you are aiming for every time you reach for your keys or money. Change your laptop's screensaver to an image of your vision. Reset your cell phone password to be something that reminds you of your vision. Place a copy of your vision inside your most-used drawer at work so that every time you open it, your North Star comes to mind. Once again, remember that what you focus on grows.

- Review your vision as often as possible, but at least once every three days. Before you do, take 60 seconds for mind rest, get present, and ground yourself in the Joy of Possibility—the energetic state of potentiality.

- As you review your vision, don't just read the words. Instead, take time to let it sink in, and experience it as real in your mind. This is important for two reasons. First, *intangible* ideas, thoughts, and beliefs create *tangible* outcomes (just like the intangible idea of an invention results in creating the tangible invention itself). Second, when you activate your imagination and bring it to life through your thoughts, beliefs, and feelings, your mind doesn't differentiate between what is real and what is imagined.

- Be *actively involved* as you walk through your vision day—in your mind's eye, in your emotions, and at the gut level— experiencing what it *feels* like to live in that desired state. Your vision day isn't taking place in the future; encounter what you are experiencing in your mind as if it's happening *right now*. When you create your vision as if it were already reality, eventually it will be.

- It's important to be "vertically aligned" as you bring your vision to life. This means making sure that how you think, feel, act, react, look, and sound *now* is 100% consistent with your vision. So as you walk through your life today, attempt as much as possible to think and feel the way you desire to think and feel during your ideal day in the future.

- Have deliberate, conscious, inner conversations that support your vision. How would you speak to yourself if you were already living your North Star existence? Refuse to engage with the Inner Defeatist in all self-talk that doesn't move you closer to your vision.

- Know and trust that your vision is unfolding. You aren't exactly sure "when" it will happen, but the key to success is to avoid getting attached to a specific date or deadline for your vision to be delivered. (That will anchor you to a fear related to the need to be right.) Instead, believe that all is working out to deliver this vision day for you when the time is right.

- Start paying close attention. As your vision begins to turn into reality, **it's very important to consistently notice when things are going well**—when events of your life align to the vision you've created. Once you consciously become aware that a part of your vision is turning out as you imagined, pause and take a moment to be grateful. This type of appreciation helps drive even greater forward-focused momentum.

Follow these guidelines, and you'll be well on your way to turning your ideal vision into reality.

—15—

How to Put This to Work for You

Let's review the core tenets we've covered in *The Forgotten Choice*:

- Energy is at the foundation of everything—both intangible and tangible—and that includes your thoughts and beliefs.

- There are two energetic states that drive two foundational thought-systems: one steeped in fear and one based on the Joy of Possibility.

- Fear never serves us—ever. But we keep choosing it, again and again, because we have so adeptly trained ourselves in fear that we don't even remember there is another option available.

- The other energetic thought-system, the Joy of Possibility, is your natural state—how you are when you strip away fear.

- Either fear or the Joy of Possibility (JOP) is at the core of every thought and belief you have.

- As the What-You-Think-Is-What-You-Get Pyramid demonstrates, your thoughts and beliefs are driving the outcomes you get. Each level within the pyramid is a response to the previous one. You have a thought and respond with a feeling. You have a feeling and respond with a behavior. Those behaviors drive the outcomes in all aspects of your life.

- Your thoughts and beliefs are reinforced by your self-talk, either through the Inner Defeatist (the voice of fear) or via the Inner Coach (the voice for the Joy of Possibility). That's why self-talk is so important—it keeps you aligned with either one or the other of the two energetic thought-systems.

- You have a choice at any moment as to which thought-system to embrace. But through years of fear-based conditioning, you've likely forgotten you have that choice.

- Through listening to self-talk, you can identify autopilot, programmed beliefs that aren't serving you—and change them. You simply have to remember this and consciously choose differently.

- To make this happen, it requires *leading* your mind. Everything starts at the level of the mind, so Mind Leadership is the single most important form of self-leadership.

- Once you recognize this and take control of your mind, you will begin to shape your outer world in the way you want. You can do this by taking mind-rest breaks, staying consciously in the present, using your anchor belief, and creating a vision of your desired life that you regularly imagine in vivid detail.

- After crafting your vision, use self-talk to reinforce new beliefs and feelings that are aligned to the Joy of Possibility. By staying vertically aligned with your vision—being consistent in how you think, feel, act, react, look, and sound—you can turn that vision into reality.

Bottom line: you were born in a state of pure, unlimited possibility with infinite potential ahead. Through learning fear, you have (unknowingly) put limits on yourself. Your life is a reflection of the choices you have made so far. If you're not 100% happy, now is the time to choose differently. You are not on this planet to be unhappy or in a state of fear. If that's the state you find yourself in, it's time to recognize that you've simply chosen that state, and you can immediately choose differently.

It's thrilling when you suddenly recognize just how *in charge* you are. But how do you truly take this information and make it work for you?

The Practicalities of the Forgotten Choice

I'm known as a pragmatic coach. I like to make things practical and immediately useful, helping clients put into place the practices and mindsets that will make change stick. Here is a page from my Coach's Playbook for how to do just that:

1) **Get clear on your level of motivation.** Sit back and ask yourself honestly: on a scale from one to ten, if one is "low" and ten is "high," what is your current level of motivation to

take all you've learned and put it into action? Based on asking this question to thousands of people around the world, if your self-score is anything lower than an eight, you'll have good intentions, but chances are high that you won't achieve what you want. You will accomplish much more with a nine or ten level of motivation.

Personally, I'm curious how anyone *wouldn't* be motivated by this. After all, the forgotten choice is the choice of a lifetime! Based on the energetic state you choose, you will either start the day with a fire in your belly or drag yourself out into the world. If you are truly motivated and can see the benefit of making these changes, you will.

One surefire way to stay motivated on a regular basis is to read your vision again and again. Once you have your ideal-day vision in your mind, to the point where you can naturally feel yourself experiencing it, your motivation level is bound to increase.

2) **Watch your mind carefully.** The most important task—where it all starts—is to pay close attention to the thoughts and beliefs that are rattling around in your head. Watch those under-the-radar, self-talk comments that impact you more than you may realize. When you notice a fear-based thought, bring it to the surface, and recognize that it's not serving you. Then choose to shift into the Joy of Possibility, immediately changing the thought to one that does serve you.

3) **Spring-clean your beliefs with a belief review.** Imagine buying the latest, most technologically advanced smartphone on the market but still carrying around your old phone with you every day. What's the point of upgrading to a better phone if you're going to insist on lugging around your old, outdated one as well?

It's the same with your beliefs. You wouldn't dream of using a mobile phone from even five years ago, but if you're like the majority of people, you have often operated your life based on beliefs that date back decades. Most, if not all, of your foundational beliefs were formed when you were much younger. They might have made sense then, helping you to understand and navigate your early years. But if you're not getting the results you want, it's time for a belief upgrade. Think of it as a shift to "Beliefs 2.0."

Granted, beliefs are far more personal than phones. And unlike mobile phones, many of your beliefs may still serve you as well today as they did the first day they were formed. For those beliefs that do continue to serve you, by all means hang on to them. But for those that no longer support you in what you want to achieve, it's time to toss them out and upgrade to thoughts that can truly help you lead the life you want.

The more willing you are to look at your beliefs and question them, the sooner your life will experience an upgrade. When a fear thought presents itself, look at it like an anthropologist would—from outside of it, in a state of objective curiosity. What belief is it reinforcing? Where did that belief come from? Is it true? If not, challenge it.

4) Take ownership of any fear-based thought or belief you experience. Regardless of where your beliefs came from, it's important to take personal responsibility for them. When you do, you can begin to choose differently and get different outcomes in life.

However, we often miss this opportunity for empowerment due to a mistaken belief that responsibility or ownership is the same as being "guilty" of something or taking blame for it.

It's easy to look back on our lives and recall some rather cringe-worthy outcomes. One of the ways we try to deal with the sting of results we don't like is to place the responsibility outside of ourselves. We look for someone or something to blame. So, it's easy to see how we've come to associate responsibility or ownership with fault and guilt.

But when it comes to your thoughts and beliefs, there doesn't have to be anybody to blame—you or anyone else. Taking ownership isn't about "who" is the cause. It's about making time to understand the energy behind what happened.

Taking ownership is positive, even exciting, because it empowers you to choose differently. After all, once you recognize a fear-based thought or belief, it's entirely up to you to keep it or not.

Until you're aware of the role beliefs play in your life, it's easy to place responsibility for outcomes on others. It's a common, knee-jerk reaction. But now that you know your beliefs are the driving force behind all that you experience, you can recognize that your beliefs are simply tales that you're free to drop or rewrite. When you do, it alters everything—your thoughts, your actions, and your ultimate results.

Blame and guilt are outdated modes of thinking used by people who are simply "managing" life—trying to keep their heads above water. However, if you're ready to lead life on your own terms, taking ownership and personal responsibility for fear-based thoughts is key to embracing the forgotten choice.

5) **Be vigilant.** You cannot be totally committed "sometimes." So, persistence is the key to success in applying the concepts shared in *The Forgotten Choice*.

Consistently pay attention to your energetic state. Check in with yourself throughout the day. Are you stressed, worried, frustrated, anxious, people-pleasing, angry, or combative? If the answer to any of these is "yes," then you'll know you are operating within the energetic state of fear. Your freedom will come through remembering that it doesn't have to be that way —that you have another option.

At the start, you may not find yourself choosing the Joy of Possibility as frequently as you'd like; in fact, you may find yourself falling back into fear fairly often. Remember: You've believed in fear for a long time now, so shifting to JOP may not feel all that natural to you, at least not initially. It may take a while to let fear go. The good news is that, at the beginning, it's enough to simply be consistently *aware* that there is a choice—a previously forgotten choice—and to begin to recognize the massive, life-affirming shift this choice can bring you.

Even if you don't choose the Joy of Possibility state all day every day, each time you're vigilant about noticing your thought-system and the role your beliefs are playing in your outcomes, you are laying the groundwork for making positive changes. And as you begin choosing JOP more frequently and naturally, it will have a direct and forward-focused impact on how your life unfolds.

6) Surround yourself with people who will support you in this change process. At the age of eight, growing up in impoverished Bangladesh, Subir Chowdhury announced to his grandfather, "One day, I will dine with the U.S. President." Without missing a beat, Subir's grandfather responded, "That sounds like a good idea." Now heralded as one of the 50 Most Influential Management Thinkers in the World and the author of 15 international bestsellers, Subir has dined not only once but *three times* with U.S. Presidents. "Dream big," Subir said when he shared this story with me.

The point of this tale may be even more powerful: think of what might have happened if Subir's grandfather had laughed and responded, "Dining with the U.S. President? Don't be ridiculous, Subir! You're a little boy from Bangladesh—that will never happen." Make sure you surround yourself with people who will support you fully as you actively choose to embrace the Joy of Possibility.

If possible, find an accountability partner, and support each other by checking in regularly about how it's going for each of you. The key to success: when choosing who to partner with, be sure to find someone equally motivated on that one-to-ten scale.

The Importance of Believing You *Can* Shift

The first step in making the all-important shift from fear-based thinking to JOP-based thinking is to embrace the *belief* that shifting is possible—knowing that you *can* choose differently, and that in doing so, you will experience change.

Some people are initially excited by the potentiality behind this shift, but then quickly fall into fear when they begin to try to make the shift.

Based on the What-You-Think-Is-What-You-Get Pyramid, this is often how it unfolds when fear is driving the show:

Think: "Changing my thoughts and beliefs is difficult."

Feel: When faced with the need for change, I feel frustrated, stuck, demoralized, and hopeless.

Behave: I lack energy, engagement, and motivation. I experience occasional outbursts of anger. My overall demeanor is negative, and I give up.

Results: Changing my thoughts and beliefs *is* difficult.

When someone consciously shifts into the JOP state and reflects on how change is possible, their pyramid shifts to read something like this:

Think: "At any moment, I can choose to change any thought or belief that limits me."

Feel: I feel a sense of liberation, freedom, and I'm determined to see the best possible outcomes.

Behave: I have an increased level of energy. I use self-talk to reinforce this foundational belief. I act in vertical alignment with my vision.

Results: I make positive, long-lasting changes in how I think and what I believe.

You Don't Need Pain to Kickstart Change

Often, we don't notice the role fear plays in our lives until we experience something that seems particularly difficult or painful. By the time that happens, chances are that fear has been building up for some time. We haven't noticed it building because we've become skilled at making adjustments when in fear, often by convincing ourselves that what's happening is "normal."

Given enough time, though, operating within the energetic state of fear starts to feel like a pressure cooker. We get so caught up in managing a situation that it's often not until things reach a boiling point that we recognize something is wrong. Then, out of desperation, we seek other, better options.

Since so much of the time our motivation to change comes in response to pain and suffering, we can mistakenly end up believing that we *need* a fear-based jolt to break out of this negative cycle. But I assure you that isn't the case. Your life doesn't have to involve a disaster or near-disaster for you to recognize that you can choose differently.

Indeed, it's never too early or too late to get out of the fear-based thought-system—no matter how extreme fear gets. You can take charge at any moment and reprogram your thinking to deliver better outcomes. You can opt to move into the Joy of Possibility starting now.

Watch your mind carefully. If you recognize that you're not in a state of JOP, then you'll know that you're listening to the Inner Defeatist and operating within the fear-based thought-system. Since the two systems are binary—you're either in one or the other—that means you're believing something that isn't true and doesn't serve you. When you recognize this, it's a monumental moment that can shift the direction of your entire life—if you let it.

Instead of waiting until life has gotten unbearable, you can remember the choice you have *now*. It doesn't matter whether you're in your teens, twenties, mid-life, sixties, eighties, or beyond—why wait?

The Importance of Consistency

Unless you're regularly and consciously aware that you are choosing between the two energetic states, your fear-based default programming will continue to run unchecked. **Until you recognize that you are free to make another choice, you will struggle in all areas of your life where your conscious desires and your outdated beliefs don't match.** And not realizing that you have a choice, you will mistakenly—and repeatedly—see yourself as a victim, blaming what is outside of you for your troubles. In doing so, you'll remain asleep to the capabilities you have within yourself to produce the outcomes you want.

Every minute of every day, this critical choice is yours. Can I personally claim that I live a life totally free of fear-based thoughts? Not 100%, but the ratio of JOP-to-fear in my life now is infinitely greater than in the past. And I easily recognize fear today and respond very quickly when a fear-based thought does rear its head. As a matter of fact, most of the time when I recognize the occasional fear thought, I end up laughing at it as I make the all-important choice to shift into the Joy of Possibility. Again, it's all about leading the mind.

So, do you want to keep living a life founded on a fear-based mindset with all of its manifestations of blame, defensiveness, worry, stress, anger, scarcity, and lack, reacting to beliefs that no longer serve you? Or are you ready to take leadership of your mind and create a life that's based on joy, creativity, and potentiality? That is the essence of the forgotten choice, and this works. In fact, it cannot fail to deliver, as long as you consistently remember and apply it.

— 16 —

The New Renaissance

The last 300 years have demonstrated our remarkable ability to create amazing "things" in our external world. The result is that our modern-day existence is in a constant state of disruption—disruption in how we communicate, how we get work done, how we shop, how we pay for goods, what we eat, how we manage our daily lives, and on and on. No aspect of our world has escaped this disruption—technology, industry, government, politics, economics, education, the home front—you name it. And the pace of disruption has gotten faster and faster to the point where, today, we are experiencing an unprecedented rate of external shift and change.

This massive disruption is all taking place *outside* of us. But as *The Forgotten Choice* has demonstrated, **what we truly need to disrupt is the one thing *inside* of us that can create real, lasting change: the way we think.**

Our present way of thinking has gotten us to where we are, but based on the survey results shared in the beginning of this book, it clearly won't get us to where we want to go. The reason we're not all dancing in the streets with joy—despite the miraculous advancements of the last few generations—is that we've mistakenly assigned our happiness to the wrong source. We keep looking outside ourselves when the real answer lies within.

Ever since the Newtonian Physics mindset discouraged us from recognizing the power of intangibles (such as the ability of thought to influence outcomes), we have collectively cut ourselves off from our true nature. Instead, we've chosen to trust in a learned, unnatural, fear-based thought-system that doesn't serve us and which has us mistakenly believing that we're incapable of creating and controlling our lives and futures.

But times have changed, and we now have the evidence to prove that what we think *is* what we get.

If you believe it's absurd to suggest that a change in your life and in our world is as simple as changing the way we think, I assure you that no real change has ever come about any other way.

No matter how strongly we hold on to old beliefs, looking outside of ourselves for solutions will never work. As much as we may desire a better experience of life for ourselves and for future generations, trying to motivate that change through fear is a losing battle. It can never result in anything except more fear. And no amount of focusing on our fears will ever resolve them— only shifting to a mindset of *possibility* can do that.

Harnessing Our Unlimited Potential

Through consciously remembering the forgotten choice, we are capable of creating our future—the relationships, careers, health, and lives we want. It's all within our internal capabilities; there's no need to search externally for it. In fact, as amazing as our external inventions have been, what we've already created outside of ourselves is only the tip of the iceberg. We haven't yet come close to harnessing our true capability.

Doing so relies on one simple yet life-altering shift of energetic state: choosing to turn away from our learned, unnatural thought-system of fear and embracing our true nature, the Joy of Possibility. **We are born with pure, unlimited potential.** It's time to turn that infinite possibility and creative energy *inward*, where it all started.

As you've gone through this book, perhaps you've been surprised to discover how many ways fear has limited you as an individual, holding you back from the day-to-day experiences you want. But now that you know the truth—that you are the cause, and the effect is the life you create for yourself—you can consciously choose to embrace the Joy of Possibility.

Because the Joy of Possibility is our natural state—the state in which we were born—**we can be living in a perpetual state of JOP, once we consistently remember the forgotten choice.**

The Vision of a JOP-Based World

In this book, we've mostly focused on the impact of choosing between fear and JOP in our *individual* lives. It's at this foundational level that all change needs to take place first.

But once we personally experience the life-altering impact of regularly operating within the JOP energetic thought-system, we can also begin to realize its potential on a much grander scale.

When you choose to be in the Joy of Possibility, there is a ripple effect. As you change your mind, your beliefs, your feelings, and your behaviors, that process automatically impacts others. I see this all the time in my coaching practice: clients make shifts in their energetic states, and their spouse, children, direct reports, colleagues, and bosses change, too. Each of us impacts the world much more than we realize.

So, remembering the forgotten choice has implications far beyond the individual. Imagine…

- parents embracing JOP-based parenting

- executives embracing JOP-based leadership

- couples embracing JOP-based relationships and JOP-based marriage

- businesses embracing JOP-based finance

- governments embracing JOP-based stewardship

Think about it: how far could this go?

What would be the impact if what is shared in this book were practiced not only at the individual or micro level, but also at the macro level—all across the planet? Consider the global outcomes of more than eight billion people all regularly choosing the Joy of Possibility.

For example, why do we live in a world with poverty where some people don't have enough food or regular access to clean water? What's holding us back?

I believe *we're not thinking big enough*. Just imagine the potential waiting to be discovered once we become aligned with the joy of Possibility. If we approach the world's problems with the right energetic base, everybody can have food. Everybody can have clean water. Everyone can live a life with "enough." It's totally doable, but not if we operate from a place of fear, stuck in beliefs that are founded in lack and limitation.

Let me put it this way: this realization isn't just bigger than we think—it's bigger than we've ever *allowed* ourselves to think.

Remembering the forgotten choice is a win-win for everybody—not just for you. Because when we are living in an energetic state of JOP, we bring about extraordinary change.

A Truth Whose Time Has Come

Consistently remembering the forgotten choice can usher in a New Renaissance: a rebirth in the way we think that allows us to embrace innovative, forward-focused beliefs. It begins with taking back leadership of our mind and making sure the thought-system we align with drives the outcomes we want—not just personally, but on a global level.

We are on the edge of a new frontier—at the cusp of potentially the most extraordinary time in human history. And it will be ushered in by consciously and steadily choosing the joy of Possibility over fear.

The faster this idea spreads, the sooner the world will change for the better. Today, the infrastructure exists that allows us to connect with anyone, anywhere in the world—a framework that can be used to support a massive increase in awareness of this empowering yet very simple choice. So the "hardware" is in place. The key now is to focus on the "software"—our minds. To take leadership of the mind and use it for good. This all begins with the individual—each one of us consistently remembering to choose JOP over fear.

The Choice is Yours

You've been reminded that the key to a happy existence lies within you, where it has always been. You have what it takes to create real, positive, and sustainable change in all aspects of your life—your relationships, marriage, family, work, career, finances, health, community, and beyond.

Now, in order to create the future you desire, it's time to fully embrace this and take ownership. All that is required is regularly remembering one, simple choice.

Pause and become aware. Ask yourself which energetic state you are in and whether that state will bring you closer to your vision day. If you're feeling anything other than the Joy of Possibility, remember that you've simply made a choice. Be kind to yourself and recall that a different choice is available to you at every moment. Then, simply choose again.

Because every time you choose the Joy of Possibility, you not only create a better life for yourself, but you make life better for all of us.

The Forgotten Choice Stories from Around the World

It's such a joy to hear from readers about how *The Forgotten Choice* has made a positive impact on their lives.

Below are a few stories and examples from readers around the world. I'd love to hear from you, too … how has *The Forgotten Choice* made a difference for you? Please feel free to share your story here: www.BrendaBence.com/myJOPstory. I look forward to hearing from you!

"As I read the book, I began to notice the truth of your message in just about every one of my thoughts and actions. I found myself not only reading *The Forgotten Choice* but practicing it on a daily basis. Out of the blue one evening, using the tools in the book, I discovered I was able to dramatically transform my state of mind—in an instant! Since then, to my profound delight, I have felt in control of areas of my life that I have always felt were out of my control. As a result, I now act more bravely, live more authentically and am carving out the path that finally feels right!"

— M. P.

"I relish the feeling of the Joy of Possibility—it's so infectious! It really *is* a choice, and while I still do find myself being in a place of fear, I remind myself how useless the fear really is, and then I feel much better immediately. I literally just used this with my husband the other day, and we managed to break the pattern/cycle with just a simple choice of not going down the usual path, along with some encouraging words anchored in JOP."

— L. H.

"Reading *The Forgotten Choice* and realizing the power we hold within has been a transformational experience for me, with significant positive impact in my life. First, I've seen phenomenal outcomes from my new team at work, thanks to my belief that they are experts at their jobs. Second, I've been battling a chronic physical condition and have been addressing it through lifestyle changes rather than relying on medication. Some months are great but during stressful months, I do see a relapse of symptoms. Thanks to *The Forgotten Choice*, I started to see that the relapses are related to the conversations I have with myself. Now, I see my condition improving every month!"

— D. J.

"Due to my hectic work schedule, I stopped baking because I just didn't have time. I was always feeling dissatisfied about this, and I blamed it on my heavy workload. Using the What-You-Think-Is-What-You-Get pyramid, I changed the way I thought about my schedule and my expectations. I threw out certain beliefs that I had (such as the need to immediately attend to every job) and made some changes to the way I work (like delegating to junior staff so they have an opportunity to develop). I also better prioritized my work and chose the Joy of Possibility, not letting the fear of work problems limit and control me. Now, I'm glad to say that I have found the time to bake again, and my kids and friends are happy that they can enjoy my baked goods again."

— S. S.

"Your book has come along at a useful time. There was an unexpected event at work which has challenged my vision. I was conscious there was likely a connection with outdated approaches or beliefs, and I was aware that my energetic state was negative. My inner voice was in 'blame' mode, which I hear most when I run. To 'self-medicate,' I switch off podcasts for half my runs to give my mind time to think in a positive, constructive manner. Thanks to your book and methodologies, I will continue to formalize my approach, which I feel is already paying dividends."

— C. G.

Thank you for reading The Forgotten Choice!

Simply by becoming aware of the potential for choosing the Joy of Possibility over fear, you've created momentum. Now, it's important to keep that momentum going.

Learning to lead your thinking is an ongoing journey. To continue moving toward the life and career you want, I encourage you to visit my website for resources to help you stay in the Joy of Possibility.

At **www.BrendaBence.com**, you'll find articles, videos, worksheets, and a community to support your progress.

I hope you will join me there!

About the Author

B renda Bence is a transformational coach who has worked with thousands of leaders across the world to help them achieve rapid, dramatic, yet sustainable success both in their professional and personal lives.

With an MBA from Harvard Business School, Brenda spent the early part of her career as a *Fortune 100* executive, leading billion-dollar brands. Upon leaving the corporate world, she started her own coaching and keynote-speaking business, which now has offices in both the U.S. and Asia. Today, Brenda is trusted by leaders from dozens of the world's largest and most recognized organizations.

As an in-demand keynote speaker, Brenda has addressed audiences across six continents, captivating people from all walks of life and motivating them toward positive, sustainable change. Sharing fascinating, real-life stories with a good dose of humor and a down-to-earth, engaging approach, Brenda has been certified by the Global Speakers Foundation as one of a small group of professional speakers who are recognized as the most successful presenters to highly diverse, multicultural audiences.

An avid author, Brenda has written 11 books that have collectively won more than 40 national and international awards. She and her work have also been featured in over 400 media outlets across the globe, such as *Inc.*, *Investor's Business Daily*, *Affluent*, *The Financial Times*, *The Los Angeles Times*, *Entrepreneur*, *Kiplinger's Personal Finance*, *Reader's Digest*, *Cosmopolitan*, and *The Wall Street Journal's Smart Money*.

Additionally, Brenda is listed as a Thinkers50 World Leader in Coaching and is consistently ranked by GlobalGurus as both a Top 10 Coach and a Top 10 Branding Expert. She has worked in or visited more than 100 countries and enjoys playing Mahjong and fuddling her way through learning new languages.

Find out more at www.BrendaBence.com

Acknowledgements

People often ask me about the process of writing books—what it takes, when I find the time to do it, how to write a book while running a business, and so on. My answer is short but honest: "Sleep is highly overrated." While intended as a joke, there is definite truth to that. Creating this book took hundreds of hours of thinking, writing, and editing. So other parts of my life were unavoidably placed on the back burner.

At the top of that "back burner list" is my husband and business partner, Daniel Jackman. You've likely heard of the loneliness of a long-distance runner, but I'm sure that pales in comparison to the loneliness of an author's spouse. Daniel showed tremendous patience for three full years as I wrote this book during every available evening, weekend, and holiday. Thank you, Daniel, as always, for your non-stop support and for always making me laugh when I need it most.

This book would not be what it is today without the contributions, support, persistence, and dedication of Sherri Rothenberger. Through dozens of late-night and early-morning calls, Sherri was there, sharing thoughts, ideas, insights, ah-ha's, edits—you name it. Our desires matched in terms of wanting to "get this right," and this process of manuscript creation took us on a journey that spanned continents and multiple time zones. Sherri, you are truly one of a kind—my jackalope—and I am blessed beyond measure to count you as a friend.

Thanks also go to Jagdish "Jag" Gill for her continuous support and willingness to explore and experiment with the various concepts of this book. Jag helped with the occasional edit, demonstrated patience during many manuscript read-throughs, and also loaned me her excellent language skills. (I still believe Jag is a closet English major.) Oh, and thanks as well, Jag, for introducing me to the concept of "madness." Very handy.

To all the family members and friends who reached out with wonderful dinner, trip, and party invitations during the writing process: please know that when I said "no," I would have liked to say "yes." But, this book had a way of convincing me otherwise. Thank you for your patience.

Appreciation also goes to the following individuals who helped me tremendously in the creation of *The Forgotten Choice*:

- Marianna Pascale, Fredrik Haren, Tom Searcy, and Carajane Moore for graciously providing feedback during the writing process—your inputs were invaluable.

- Melanie Votaw for her expert guidance and advice in the editing process—I value our long-term partnership.

- Jessi Rita Hoffman for her keen eye and expert editing skills.

- Swas "Kwan" Siripong for interior graphics and visuals.

- Eric Myhr for his always excellent typesetting services and "can-do" attitude.

Lastly, many thanks to Dr. Sue Morter, author of *The Energy Codes*, for taking time to provide consultation on the subjects of physics and energy. I appreciate your support.